THE UNSHAKEABLE
ROAD TO LOVE

(VALUE-CENTERED RELATIONSHIPS)

Brenda Shoshanna

DEDICATION

This book is dedicated to my incredible brother, Daniel Myerson, who is a living example of truly living a life of love. He has been an unfailing source of support, strength and inspiration throughout the writing of this book and through all the years. Throughout his life Daniel has been steadfast in his spiritual life and in manifesting its highest principles in all situations. A brilliant, independent thinker, Daniel's joy and deep connection to those from all countries and styles of life, and his true caring for others, have been an incredible reminder of what truly matters.

ACKNOWLEDGMENTS AND THANKS

There are so many people I wish to thank for their support, caring, and inspiration. I give great thanks to my wonderful family, Melissa, Joshua, Adam and Noah, and their families for the hours of delight, guidance and support. Thanks also goes to dharma brother Martin Hara and the wonderful Rinzai zendo he works so hard to support throughout the years.

For assisting me with practice and dharma work in all kinds of ways. I wish to thank Fr. Kennedy Roshi for his unfailing strength, support, kindness and dedication, and also thank and acknowledge all of his wonderful sangha including Joann Miller, Russ Michel, Carl Vigianni and Amy Yee. Great thanks also for the abiding friendship of Faye Tabakman, Michael Klein, Bernie Starr and Richard Schiffman throughout so many years.

TABLE OF CONTENTS

INTRODUCTION

"The Whole World Is Medicine.
What Is the Illness?"

We are all treasure hunters, looking for the secret to fulfilling relationships. Usually, we believe the secret lies in finding the right person, acquiring the best relationship skills and learning to communicate our needs more clearly. Our relationships are usually dedicated to finding happiness, getting our needs met, being powerful or in charge. Basically, we are using our relationships to feel good about ourselves.

However, despite all our efforts, relationships often become a source of pain and suffering. Conflict, anger, disappointment and loneliness arise endlessly. And many times, when a partner stops supplying our needs, what felt like love one day turns to rejection the next.

When our thoughts are primarily absorbed with what we are needing and receiving, or how to build ourselves up, we live in a prison without bars. Due to our absorption with ourself, it becomes impossible to truly see the person we are with, or what is going on in front of our eyes. Any slight, real or imagined, can become the cause of distress, causing us to withdraw. Any perceived failure or rejection invites underlying feelings of worthlessness to emerge, producing additional depression and stress. The harder we try to make things right, the more complicated they can become. How can we ever find fulfillment in this manner?

Know the Difference Between Medicine and Poison

"The way out is through the door,
How come nobody ever takes that method?"

There is a great deal of confusion these days about what causes mental, emotional and physical illness and how suffering can be healed. Most psychotherapy focuses upon our personal history, emotions, fixed habits and cognitive responses. However, even when a person feels better, new symptoms and problems endlessly appear. While psychotherapy can certainly be helpful, the root of our illness has not been touched. We are more than our history, memories, emotions, desires, needs, habits and cognitive patterns we have formed.

Despite all the efforts of psychology and therapy, we have not been able to alleviate the true illness, loneliness, deception and a profound sense of disconnection, both from others and ourselves. Withdrawal and pretense are so pervasive that they are even taken as the norm. Deep contentment and meaning remain elusive.

In many cases these treatments are built upon rejection of the very truths that provide true meaning to our lives. When we base our lives and relationships upon fashionable, though faulty, principles, pain and confusion intensify. As a result, addiction to drugs, medicine and treatments of all kinds have never been so pervasive. Nor the suffering still so great. The emptiness we live with must be addressed differently.

Misguided treatments can easily encourage more self-absorption, blame of others and false identities. So often we come away from one another filled with misunderstanding and confusion. This is simply due to the many walls we have erected against truly being known and knowing our whole, undivided selves.

Most of us don't know the difference between poison and medicine. We engage in poisonous behavior and expect our lives and relationships to be healthy and strong. What is passed off as medicine is often poison, ultimately lethal for us. And the true medicine is readily available, wherever we are. We only have to discover what it is and how to take it.

A Completely New Perspective

It is time to offer a completely new perspective on psychological and spiritual suffering and health, and how to practice this new perspective in our everyday lives. The essence of our being is filled with the wisdom and healing that we are searching for everywhere else.

As we turn to the world's Eternal Scriptures we see that suffering has been dealt with throughout the centuries. All world scriptures ask us to stop a moment and examine the essential cause of our suffering, and the real medicine for it. However, this fundamental, eternal wisdom has not been recognized or invited into our relationships. That is why we suffer so.

As we turn to the world's scriptures we discover profound relationship insights along with powerful forms of healing offered again and again. These teachings are grounded in the basic spiritual truths that govern our lives and relationships.

A Radical Alternative

An Unshakable Road To Love (Value-Centered Relationships) is based upon eternal truths found in all world scriptures. These principles provide the perfect remedy for all that causes pain. Not only are these principles fundamental to our happiness, they are also simple, easy to understand and enjoyable to perform. They are the perfect medicine for what is truly ailing us.

These truths present a radical alternative to the ways we function in relationships and what we expect of them. Like the laws of gravity, these principles are infallible, cannot fail. Yet, we have not taken them to heart or practiced them in our lives.

However, when these eternal principles are understood, lived and turned to regularly, it is startling to see how quickly our mental, emotional and even physical suffering dissolves. Their focus, direction and way of being not only protect us from hurt and upset, but provide great fulfillment and stability in all situations. It is amazing how quickly we can see the truth and respond in a beneficial way for all.

True Medicine Is Delicious

This book and program are dedicated to sharing a new form of psychology based upon these Eternal Principles.

This is a book of practice, simple, direct and filled with specific, Pillars of Love, Turning Points and Exercises so that we may practice these truths all day long, with whomever we meet, including ourselves.

As we do, we will be astonished to see that true medicine is delicious. These practices are simple, enjoyable and incredibly powerful. They bring immediate change as the conflict, bitterness and loneliness we live with daily dissolve. When these principles and practices are understood and practiced it is startling to see how enjoyable they are and how quickly our emotional and physical suffering turns around. And how these principles benefit all.

Turning Points

Turning Points are actions, perceptions and responses based upon the Pillars of Love. They interrupt our usual way of seeing and doing things and provide specific interventions to practice with everyone we encounter. As we do so, upset and pain disappear on the spot. The conflict that has been going on between us and others can easily melt away.

These principles focus our energy, prevent us from *reacting* in a knee-jerk manner and make room for us to *respond* instead. They stop us from becoming embroiled in negativity, or in the grip of heartbreak and despair.

A Book of Practice: Open Your Own Treasure House

This book is a guide to help you through the stumbling blocks and mazes that surround love. The practices will help you roll one stumbling block after another out of the way. Do them again and again, digest and assimilate them into your life. Go at your own pace. Each practice is simple, yet powerful. Some will fit more for you than others, and that's fine.

As you engage in this process, you will notice that you are feeling stronger, more centered, alive, valuing each day more and more.

What you are now doing is opening your own treasure house. You are tapping into the incredible reservoir of wisdom waiting within. As you do so, your own inner guidance becomes activated and you will also discover many other inner treasures you've never been aware of before. This is an exciting journey to embark upon; it will uplift all aspects of your life.

Relationship Koans

Open Your Own Treasure House is a koan. All relationships can be thought of as koans, teachings coming to us from the world of Zen. It is extremely liberating to view your relationship that way. A koan is a question given to a student by a teacher that has no logical or rational answer. And yet an answer must be made. The student's very life is at stake if they do not respond. The same is true of relationships.

When we start working on koans, naturally we try to figure them out, determine the odds, strategize, demand certain outcomes. We approach our koans as we do our relationships. Before long it is easy to see how limited and distressing that way is. How it ties us into endless knots.

Relationship Myths and Mirages

As we work on our relationship koans, it is easy to see many of the illusions we have been living with, and how they have destroyed our joy. These illusions, or mirages, are myths about others, ourselves and what love really is.

These myths and mirages steal our trust, hope and direction. They prevent us from seeing the difference between poison and medicine, and cause suffering in all aspects of our lives.

Working on Our Koan (Instruction):

Ultimately, we do not work on our koans, they work on us. Koans call other parts of our being into play, alter our perspective and present possibilities we never imagined were there. This is true of our relationships as well. Relationships, truly understood and practiced, are not only profound spiritual practice, they are an incredible gateway into the heart of our lives.

Here is a wonderful instruction given to students working with a koan. It is wonderful instruction for being in a relationship as well.

Be With Your Koan as if You Were a Mother Hen Sitting On Her Nest, Keeping Her Eggs Warm. (Do the Same with Your Relationship.)

Don't leave the nest or desert the chicks. And don't interfere by constantly peeking in to see how the chicks are doing, or pushing them to grow. When the perfect moment comes the chicks will peck out of their shells and be born. Do the same with your relationship!

Stay centered and present throughout all conditions. Be there, providing stability and warmth. And don't interfere with the growth of the person or of the relationship by constantly checking it and pushing things to grow. Trust the organic nature of life to guide the process. When the right moment comes, just like the chick, the relationship will become fully alive.

Each Pillar of Love in Value-Centered Relationships is like a little chick, waiting to grow and to be born in your life. It needs attention, warmth and steadiness as you absorb and practice it. Then, when you are ready, at the right moment, all is revealed.

Through this book we will explore the different koans our relationships are presenting to us. As we apply the Pillars of Love and Turning Points, we are allowing for the love waiting within to be born. All the answers and guidance are waiting inside you. Let them be revealed.

During This Journey You Will

Discover the Difference Between Real and
Counterfeit Love

Uncover and Live the Timeless Truths of Love

Know the Difference Between Poison and
Medicine

Give Up Poisonous Food Where It Is Offered
to You

Learn How to Truly Give and Receive

Welcome the Silence

Engage in True Conversations

Taste and See That Life Is Good

"Kabir says, Fantastic!
Don't let an opportunity
Like this go by."

SECTION ONE

PREPARING FOR THE JOURNEY

"Where Is The Road
To Hanshan?
There Is No Road
To Hanshan."

CHAPTER 1

Starting Out
Dedicating Your Relationships

"Where is the road
To Hanshan?
There is no road
To Hanshan."

What Are Your Relationships Dedicated To?

Where Is the Road to Hanshan?

Where are we going in our relationships? What is our destination? Most of the time we have no idea. Our relationships are not based upon anything in particular. We are often just ambling along with no idea of the outcome waiting up ahead. Other times we set out on the road to Hanshan, with all kinds of dreams, fantasies and expectations. What a shock to realize that the road to Hanshan may not even exist. What we're hoping for is a mirage.

Usually our relationships just happen by happenstance. We meet someone and experience all kinds of reactions, some of which can be very strong. It's as though a sudden wind comes out of nowhere, tosses us around and we're blown like a leaf off a tree. This sudden wind is fueled by the many fantasies, memories and hidden desires that are arising. Deep within we may think, *I've finally met person of my dreams who is going to meet all my needs.*

No One Has to Meet Your Needs

There's an implicit belief that a person you're in a relationship with has to meet your needs. Who said so? This demand itself is the cause of so much heartbreak and pain. And it is based upon a false assumption that another can make you truly happy or fill up the emptiness within.

We often hear someone say that I'm finished with this relationship because it doesn't meet my needs. (We seldom say I'm finished with these needs because it doesn't serve the relationship.)

The desire to have someone else meet your needs does damage in so many ways. It turns your relationships into transactions. Now you are in the orientation of the marketplace, which closes the door to really knowing the other, to a deep connection and experience of love.

Transactional Relationships

A transactional relationship is based upon barter: you give me what I want, and I'll give you what you want in return. If the person fulfills your demands, they are worthwhile and you'll keep them around. Once they do not meet your expectations, they are often discarded. You have turned the person into an object to meet your needs. Their value to you is based upon what you're getting out of the relationship. This orientation can only bring sorrow and pain.

Pillar of Love: Do Not Make the Other an Object to Meet Your Needs.

When you demand that another person be there for you, make you happy, this has nothing to do with love. When we turn another person into an object, we can never know who they truly are, who is standing before us. We miss the incredible opportunity for the communication and connection we so deeply long for. And we are living in direct opposition to a Pillar of Love.

Another Person Can Not Make You Happy or Unhappy

Fundamentally, another person cannot make you either truly happy or unhappy. When you feel happy and complete in the relationship it is because you are living in accordance with a Pillar or Principle of love. It is the arising of love that is making you feel happy and fulfilled.

When you are feeling upset, lonely or discontented in a relationship, your sorrow is due to living in opposition to a Pillar of Love. Your perspective is then distorted and you are going against fundamental values and principles that inevitably bring joy. No matter what happens in the relationship, it is your perspective itself, where you stand, that will cause either pain or joy.

"The Road Is Made By Walking On It."

Eduardo

Sacred Encounters

Although we may not know the road to Hanshan (not know where we are going), we create the path of our relationships by the steps we take, day by day. And the foundation of the road we walk along is supported by what our relationship is dedicated to. We can go around and around, waiting for our needs to be met, or point the relationship in a new direction.

A relationship contains enormous possibilities. It can become a sacred place, a temple, a sanctuary, a home for growth, love and trust. Ultimately, the relationship can become a place to encounter the divine, or a place for a real meeting to take place. Relationships are true spiritual practice when viewed this way.

Relationships as Spiritual Practice

A story in the Torah offers wonderful guidance to what it possible. The story describes a couple greatly rejoicing at their wedding, delighted that they have found the One. With all the excitement, they feel that they are at the peak of their love. How can it get any better than this? they wonder.

But the Torah says, No! This is not the high point, or the peak of your love. Finding your partner, your marriage, is only the beginning. Your partner is your teacher in what it means to love.

This is such a startling and profound teaching. It applies not only to a marriage partner, but to everyone you meet. How incredible our lives would be if we could view every person who comes into our world as our Teacher in what it means to love. And how true it is.

As we change the lens through which we see others, they feel it and respond in kind. We invite certain kinds of behavior in others by the way we see and respond to them.

Pillar of Love: Everyone You Meet Is Your Teacher in Learning What It Means To Love.

Turning Point: In Your Mind, Thank Each Person You Meet for Being Your Teacher In What It Means to Love.
Every encounter you have is an incredible opportunity to learn, grow, connect, be joyous and infuse meaning into your life. This is even true with someone who might initially seem like a casual acquaintance.

Is There Such a Thing as a Casual Acquaintance?

"This moment will not come again."

Eido Roshi

What makes a person a "casual acquaintance"? It is simply the way we view and relate to them. Often, we label a person and relate to their label, not to them. We're relating to a fantasy we have about the person, when we have no idea who they really are. What a missed opportunity. We never saw who was really there, and what was possible between us, even for a moment or two.

Are we seeing a person as they were a few months ago, with no idea of who they are right now? Each moment and person are fresh and unique. Everyone blooms when they are truly seen.

Are we willing to stop in front of the doorman, postman, or clerk and see that they are much more than their label, take a moment and give them a real smile and hello?

Treat Everyone In Your Life as Valued and Hallowed

Fortunately, it is a simple matter to replace the error. As we begin to view and treat everyone in our lives as valued, hallowed, and significant just as they are, that is how others will begin to feel. And also to respond to us. There is then no limit to the possibilities of healing, love and well-being for all. Try and see.

"Heaven Is Not Somewhere You Go
It's Something You Carry Within You."

Lubavitch Rebbe

Pillar of Love; Who Is Honored? He/She Who Honors Others

We all want to be respected and honored and wonder why it may not take place. In the Wisdom of the Fathers the question arises, Who Is Honored? And the answer is clear and unfailing. *He Who Honors Others.* This wonderful guidance breaks into our self-absorption and shows the path to unfailing respect from others, but self-respect as well.

It's impossible to disrespect ourselves when we know we are acting in accordance with the deeper laws of love.

Try and see. Are you viewing the person as someone to meet your needs or as someone worthy of honor?

Turning Point: View Each Person You Interact With as Someone Worthy of Honor

Now you are aligning yourself with the deepest truth of each person. And the way you view a person will affect the way you behave; the tone of your voice, the look in your eyes. It will also affect the way they respond.

See the person before you as worthy of honor before you interact. Change the lens through which you look and your entire world changes as well.

Practice: Treat Everyone in Your Life as Valued and Hallowed

As we begin to view and treat everyone in our lives as valued, hallowed, and significant just as they are, that is how others will begin to feel. And it is also how they will respond to you. There is then no limit to the possibilities of healing, love and well-being for all. Try and see.

    A) Take a moment to see what it is that makes you feel honored.

    B) Then behave that way with the other.

There is so much joy waiting for you when you are ready to receive it. Why not be ready today?

Turning Point: Building a Strong Foundation

Dedicate Your Relationships

Now it is time to stop and take a look at our own lives. In order to change the course of our relationships, to enter the Unshakable Road to Love, the first step is to be aware of where we are now, and then Dedicate Our Relationships to a new destination.

An architect would never build a building without a solid foundation. He needs strong pillars and also needs to know where they belong. If there is no foundation, when a storm comes along, the building will crash down. The same is true of a relationship. When we learn how to build strong foundations, dependent upon the Pillars of Love, our relationships will be able to withstand the many storms that inevitably come along.

These storms can actually make the relationship stronger, strengthen our understanding of the nature of love. The Pillars of Love build our relationships upon a foundation that provides true shelter and strength. They allow us to create relationships which can become a sanctuary, a true home.

Building an Unshakable Foundation

Dedicating Your Relationships is a way to anchor yourself in truth. No matter what is happening, it is fully within your ability to dedicate yourself to learning and living the truth about love. A dedication is an aspiration, a commitment, a direction. When you dedicate your relationship, you are no longer at the mercy of passing events or people, but are anchored in your own truth. You occupy your own reality, do not get pulled into all the passing emotions and narratives that come along.

Before we dedicate our relationships it is important to examine our own lives, see where we are now, and what our true direction is.

Practice: What Foundation Is Your Relationship Based Upon?

Write down what your relationships dedicated to. What are you looking for?

What do you want to receive?

What are you willing to give?

Who brings forward the best in you?

What are your relationships based upon?

Review your relationships. Why are you in them? Why did they end, or last as long as they did? A relationship can unknowingly be based upon many things that will never allow the relationship to grow or provide the fulfillment desired.

There may be serious cracks in the foundation, or the reasons you are together, that will not support the relationship in the long run.

Is the relationship dedicated to meeting your needs, making you happy, feeling safe and worthwhile? Just take note. Soon you will see why this kind of dedication will never hold up. It is based upon Myths and Mirages about relationships, also called Counterfeit Love.

Practice: Relationship Dedications

Here are some other ways to view and dedicate your relationships. All of these are based upon the Pillars of Love. If the focus in your relationships is primarily to feel good and comfortable, why not dedicate the relationship to making the other feel comfortable and good?

A) Dedicate the relationship to Giving, not Getting.

B) Dedicate the relationship to Growing in Love.

C) Dedicate the relationship to Wonderful Discoveries.

D) Dedicate the relationship to Empowering Others to Grow Strong.

E) Dedicate the relationship to being a Sanctuary, a Temple.

Find a Dedication that feels just right to you.

Dedicate All Your Relationships to Practicing the Pillars of Love

No matter how you feel, you are always in charge of what you focus on. You can choose to get pulled into an old pattern or to use the moment to bring growth, light, and love. Once you do this, you are not at the mercy of passing feelings or circumstances. You are taking a stand for what is meaningful, and how *you will respond.* Dedicating Your Relationships is a way to anchor yourself in truth. No matter what is happening, it is fully within your ability to dedicate yourself to learning and living the truth about love.

Whenever something happens that is distressing, immediately remind yourself of your dedication and a Pillar of Love. Take one of the Turning Points and act upon it.

When asked in the Torah how we can know these teachings are true, the reply came.

Do and You Will See.

You are not asked to believe anything here, just practice these principles day after day. Once action is taken, you will see the effect. And as you keep taking action, much will be revealed to you. These practices are easy to do and you will feel so good as you keep doing them. Soon it will be impossible to return to the old bumpy roads.

Practice: Before You Begin an Interaction, Remember What Your Relationships Are Dedicated to. Focus on That.

Plant Yourself as a Pillar of Love.

CHAPTER 2

Relationship Mirages
Undoing Counterfeit Love

"The great doors remain closed
But the spring fragrance
Comes inside anyway."

Kabir

The great doors that are closed are the doors of our hearts. Yet despite our hardness and resistance, the fragrance of love enters anyway, and suddenly, we are touched.

We all want love. Then, when we get it, we become afraid and start to run in the opposite direction. On the one hand, we are searching for love, searching for some lasting relationship.

On the other hand, we are relieved when the person goes away. It always "seems" as if relationships are difficult. They are difficult to find, difficult to keep and difficult to enjoy.

Yet, the fundamental truth is:

There is no inherent problem with relationships at all.

There Is Never a Scarcity of Relationships
There Is Never a Scarcity of Love
Love Is Our Natural Condition
Why aren't we in it all the time? What is it that
  keeps us from this love we are so hungry for?

Finding the Perfect Person

The most common answer to this question is that first we must find The Perfect Person. There is always something wrong with the people we meet. We have not yet found the "right" person, who can make us really happy, show us how to sing.

Or, if we have found The Perfect Person, they have now left us, and we believe nobody will ever take their place again. At this point we still believe that another person can make us happy. About to take our journey, we may wonder how to find the right partner to travel with. Without someone beside us, we may feel empty and alone.

The Craving to Be Loved

Most are unhappy in relationships because they crave to be loved, to have their sense of self-importance affirmed. They keep this search going and are disappointed again and again. This is a quest for validation in the eyes of another. If this approval is not forthcoming, they feel like failures. Their very sense of who they are becomes tied to the moods and behavior of others. This orientation will never bring balance or a true sense of worth.

However, most of us live in fear of blame, censure and rejection. We feel that to be happy we must be approved of, receive praise and recognition. But even when we receive a great deal of approval for a period of time, when it is gone, the craving for it grips us once again.

This is not because there is something wrong with us. It is simply due to the fact that we have not yet understood the true nature of love. We're caught in a maze of mirages, under the grip of Counterfeit Love.

Turning Point: The Longing for Approval Is an Addiction

However, the longing for approval is an addiction. The more we get, the more we want. Approval never fills us up completely and it never will, because approval is a form of *Counterfeit Love.* And the moment we no longer receive approval from our partner, our so-called love for them often turns into anger and fear.

Many of us limit ourselves due to the craving for approval and praise. We live our lives in dread of blame, censure and rejection. Our basic relationship goal is to be loved.

Pillar of Love: To Be Happy, We Do Not Have to Be Loved, We Must Learn to Be Loving.

When we are truly loving, we feel loved and worthy. This kind of love does not falter or pass away with every changing mood. It is the essence of who we are and the more we give of it, the more we are filled. All that we have ever wanted is fully available to us when we don't get caught in confusion and learn and practice the Truths about Love.

It Is Impossible to Be Loving and Upset at the Same Time

Once we learn the difference between Real and Counterfeit Love it is easy to see that on the road to Unshakeable Happiness we do not need to be loved, but to be loving. All the pain in relationships is simply due to our being caught in Counterfeit Love. It is the mirages, illusions and false expectations we have about love and relationships that break our heart in two. These myths and mirages are so pervasive that most have no idea why their relationships keep going wrong, time and again.

Pillar of Love: Real Love Never Hurts or Wounds. If It Does, It's Counterfeit Love.

Counterfeit Love is the idea that love is an emotion, excitement, infatuation or strong feeling of attachment. In counterfeit love if we feel strongly toward someone, need them, we immediately assume that we are in love. When we feel happy with them, at ease, cared for or connected, we feel we've found what we're searching for.

Counterfeit Love Is
Believing That Love Is Excitement, Infatuation or Feelings of Need
Creating An Ideal or Fantasy and Falling in Love with That
Confusing the Craving for Approval with Love

Turning a Person into an Object to Meet Our Needs
Wanting to Dominate or Control, or to Be Dominated and Controlled
Using a Relationship for Status, Security or Feelings of Self
Undoing Counterfeit Love

"A Feeling That Is Here One Moment
And Gone the Next
Cannot Be Called Love."

Love Is Not A Feeling

Feelings are fleeting. It is their very nature to come and go. As all feelings must change, many believe that love cannot last. They do not realize that love is not a feeling. Real love can never leave. But as it is the nature of feelings to change, that is also the nature of Counterfeit Love.

Real love is not based upon passing emotion. There is not a rejection of another person if they do not meet your needs. Real love is not a feeling to cling to. It is the very foundation upon which we live. As we learn how to build that foundation our footsteps become planted on the Unshakeable Road To Love.

Feelings Are Fleeting

When we base a relationship upon that which fluctuates, we become stressed and insecure. We do not realize that we are simply depending upon passing feelings to give us a sense of happiness and worth. But as these passing feelings fluctuate, so does our sense of being in love. When the feelings become unpleasant, we often leave the relationship as soon as we can. Many say the relationship was wonderful in the beginning, but after a while everything changed. Distraught, they ask where did the love go? Of course the love didn't go anywhere, because it wasn't love in the first place.

However, a common illusion is that there is a Perfect Person waiting somewhere, and once we find them, all will be well.

This sense of being incomplete, and of having to cling to a Perfect Person (or image), is bound to bring sadness and fear. If we do not feel secure within ourselves, is it really so surprising that we may not really be so eager after all for this Perfect Person to appear at our door?

When we feel we are "not good enough," and that we desperately "need" another, we are not yet able to love. But be cheered:

Pillars of Love

We Are Always Good Enough.

We Are Always Complete.

Love Is Free, It Flows Everywhere.

It flows to everyone regardless of their qualities.

Why are you keeping it away?

The Search for the Perfect Person

Many live with the idea that when they find the perfect person they'll finally be able to love. Sadly, this widespread relationship mirage causes much disarray. This search can become both an addiction and an excuse not to open our hearts to the person who is right here. It's helpful to explore who the perfect person is for you. Who are you waiting for in order to be able to love?

Practice: Who Is the Perfect Person?

Take a moment to write *all* the qualities your perfect person would have. Now, write down how you would have to be in order to have such a partner.

Just doing this exercise, you may begin to laugh. There may be wild discrepancies in how you see yourself now, and how you feel you have to be to keep such a Perfect Partner at Your Side.

The image of the Perfect Person dominates our lives in so many ways. We set up all kinds of expectations about how they must be. Then when they fall short of our demands, all kinds of pain occurs. (We do this with ourselves as well.)

The Perfect Person can also be called our Social Self, the image we seek to project, the mask we wear that keeps us hidden and lonely as we face the world.

What Else Might You Discover?

You might also discover that you do not really like this Perfect Person after all. They may only be some kind of ego ideal (someone to build up your own self-image).

When we use another person to build up our own self-image, this kind of relationship is grounded in fear. Without this person we might feel as if we were nothing, or as if our lives were meaningless. Then we blame the other for not making us feel better about ourselves, or feeling secure.

Making Sure Love Won't Happen

Being with someone we feel is perfect can make us even more painfully aware of our own imagined inadequacies. Deep down we feel that this relationship can't last because we do not really deserve it. Sooner or later, this Precious Person is bound to find out who we "really" are. Then they will surely leave.

Practice: What Would Happen if One Day the Perfect Person Suddenly Walked into Your Life?

What kind of responses might then occur? Here are some ways you might feel.

What can they possibly see in me?

How can I ever hold them?

How awful will it be when they reject me, as I know they eventually must?

What happens if we do have a relationship and I'm still not happy after all?

It's common to blame the other for the pain we are in. We also blame ourselves and declare that relationships are inherently painful. A great fear of love is caused by the imagined hurt and pain it's bound to cause. We fear how difficult it will be when we lose our love, or are rejected. Due to this fear some become unable to enter a relationship again. They withdraw in order to protect themselves from the hurt and disappointment they say love brings.

But this fear is simply caused by the lack of under-standing of the true nature of relationships and love.

Pillar of Love: Each Person Is the Perfect Person for You to Love.

The Perfect Person for you to love is the one who is standing in front of you, right now. Here, right where you are.

Turning Point: Choose to Say Yes

What and who do you say yes to unreservedly? Who do you refuse? Why?

"I could have loved you,
but I won't!
First you got to Love Me!!"

Practice: Who Wants Your Love?

Who is in your life now? Who wants your love?

Look Around for a Moment. Really Look at This Person.

Are You Willing to Love Them Just as They Are?

What has to change about them for you to love them? What has to change about you?

Will You Allow Them to Love You Too?

Love is free, it flows everywhere
It flows to everyone, regardless of their qualities.

CHAPTER 3

The Precious Jewel

"The precious jewel we have lost
Some say it is to the east of us
Others to the west."

Rumi

Where Is the Precious Jewel?

Most of us feel that something important is missing in our lives and we run all over, searching for it. Some travel to meet great teachers, while others search for this jewel in relationships. Many feel that the precious jewel is their soul mate, someone waiting for them in the world out there.

However, this beautiful poem suggests that our deepest heart and fulfillment will not be found out on the highways and byways, either to the east or west. The precious jewel is not something to be acquired, used, or played with. It is always waiting for us, within.

There's a wonderful story of Enyadatta who was very ill and became desperate feeling that she'd lost her head. And she couldn't find it. Around and around she ran searching for her head, until suddenly during a startling moment she realized it had never been lost at all. There it was, right on her shoulders.

Reclaiming Oneself

Most of us are terrified to claim our own life back, look through our own eyes, live from the truth of who we are. We question ourselves and our perceptions constantly. We are not willing to walk on this earth with our own two feet, to live the life given to us. We become cardboard figures, imitations of everyone else.

As we reclaim our own selves, we are not deceived or trapped by others. And we no longer disconnect from our treasure within.

Turning Point: Look Through Your Own Eyes

Take your own life back. Look through your own eyes. See life fresh and new the way you alone can see it. Pause and pay attention to what you see and feel. Value that.

As we run around seeking love and connection, we don't know what we're really looking for. But what we are missing and seeking is right here. It's ourselves. We also fervently seek connection with another, but even when we find it, we may have no idea who's really there.

Falling in Love with a Fantasy

It's easy to fall in love with our dreams about our partner. In the beginning the dream feels wonderful and the beauty of it reflects upon us. How wonderful we must be to have a partner like this!

Then reality sets in. Sooner or later, difficulties arise and we are forced to see other aspects of the person, and other aspects of ourselves as well. When we don't like what see, we blame it on them, cry out that they've deceived or betrayed us.

But the truth is we never really knew them. We've only known our dreams about them.

How Can He Do This to Me?

Years ago, I discovered something shocking about a person I looked up to, spent a great deal of time with, and adored. The shock took over me for a while and one day I mentioned it to a mutual friend.

"I loved him so much. How could he do this to me?" I said, in tears.

The friend looked at me clearly. "He didn't do anything to you!" he replied. "In fact, you didn't love him at all, you just loved your fantasy about him. You never even knew him. When you can know everything about a person and still love them, that is love."

My friend's words startled me deeply. I recognized their incredible truth, and at that moment a dedication in my life and relationships became to know everything I could about someone, and love them fully.

Pillar of Love: When You Know Everything about a Person and Still Love Them, That Is Love.

It's easy to be in love when the person seems to be the one of your dreams. However, when you know the full truth about someone (even if it is not to your liking) and still care for them, then you're really doing something.

"When we see truly, we can live truly."

Emerson

Allowing Change to Happen

"If I haven't seen you for three days, it cannot be said I know you."

Really knowing someone includes allowing them to grow and change. We keep others stuck by seeing them in the same old way, refusing to relate to the changes they've gone through.

If you haven't seen the person for three days, they are not the person you knew before. Change is constant and unavoidable. In all relationships we set up an idea or image about who the person is and how they must remain. But the relationship cannot be static, as the person doesn't belong to us, they belong to time.

Everything changes constantly, including the people we are close to. Do we allow the change or even realize it's happening? Or do we see the person as they were months or weeks ago? Are we holding the person in a fixed image in our minds? If so, we do not know them, but only know our images and fantasies about them. And this fixation impedes the flow of true connection and the experience of real love.

Turning Point: Wake Up to the Freshness of Every Moment

It is crucial to be awake to the freshness of all of life and allow ourselves and others to be new. If we cannot, we are out of touch with what that person truly needs from us now. And, inadvertently, we may be holding someone in a negative pattern they have outgrown.

Pillar of Love: Grant Each Person the Right to Be Who They Are.

Turning Point: Let Go of Your Images of Others, See Who Is Really There

A deep act of love is to grant each person the right to be who they are. A person is here to learn, grow, and fulfill their own destiny, not to fit into some image you have of them. Step back a moment and enjoy their adventure. See the larger vista and give all room to change and grow.

Practice: In Your Mind Say to All You Meet, I Grant You the Right to Be Who You Are.

If something disturbing happens between you, rather than jumping in and correcting, blaming or rejecting them, say in your mind: I Grant You the Right To Be Who You Are.

This simple statement, when said from the heart, is extremely powerful, and will immediately end your uproar and distress. Once the uproar within quiets down, not only will the other feel it, but you will discover a new depth between you. You'll be on the road to truly meeting and knowing the person, not your dream of him.

Pillar of Love: Anything We Can't Love or Accept In Another Is a Mirror of Something We Can't Accept in Ourselves.

Realize that you have attracted this person in order to see yourself a little better. What you reject in another you are also rejecting in yourself. When we're unwilling to love, we find all kinds of excuses for it by blaming it on the other person and rejecting them. But this is only the fear of love speaking, confusing and distorting our point of view.

Pillar of Love: Love Is the Acceptance of Ourselves and Others Just as We Are.

This pillar of love is a lifelong practice and journey. Inevitably we will be confronted with qualities and behaviors in others and ourselves that we cannot accept.

The Practice of Acceptance

Acceptance does not mean to support behavior that you find reprehensible. It means to see what is truly happening without getting caught in the whirl. In the process you step back and give the person space to go through whatever is happening for them, not making it about you. You are allowing them to grow and for things to naturally change.

Acceptance never means staying in a toxic situation or letting go of standards. As you see things as they are, it's natural to take appropriate action that is beneficial for all.

The practice of acceptance is so necessary as there is part of ourselves that is programmed to constantly criticize, blame, reject. This is a great disease of the mind. This part of ourselves can be called ego, monkey mind, or that which sabotages life and love. As this disease is counteracted, we no longer participate in its madness, but instead return to love.

The Disease of the Mind

"To Separate What We Like from What We Do Not Like Is the Disease of The Mind."

Sosan

From the moment we wake up in the morning until we go to sleep, we are busy rejecting what life has to offer. We are constantly accepting some experiences and clinging to them and throwing away many others. Indeed, rejection can be thought of as "the disease of the mind." We refuse to taste so much of life, constantly judge and condemn others and refuse love if a person doesn't make the grade.

When we live our lives searching for and clinging to what we want and rejecting the rest, this tears us in half. We live in constant dread of something happening and constant longing for something else. This also uses up our precious energy. Half of our life energy is used rejecting the world. The other half is used seeking for and grasping at that which we desire. Living this way, how can we be available to that which is being given to us, that which is truly present, what our life consists of today? And how can we be free of the poison of the anger which arises when we aren't able to have or hold onto what we want?

Who Made Us the Judge and Jury?

To separate what we like from what we dislike kills all relationships both with others and with ourselves. We love one and hate another; we admire the rich and step over the homeless. We look up at the masters, and down at beginning students. We sit in judgment upon all of life, never stopping to ask ourselves, who are we to judge anyone? Who made us judge and jury?

Can we truly be so arrogant to judge and reject this immense world that has been given to us to care for and love? Have relationships been given to us to dispose of harshly, or to nourish? In order to taste the beauty and joy of life we must turn this usual way of behaving around one hundred and eighty degrees.

Turning Point: Do Not Separate What You Like from What You Dislike

When we meet with someone noisy, rude or unpleasant, this is a wonderful opportunity. Rather than push the person aside, it is the perfect time to practice not separating what you like from what you dislike.

Accept that person and be with him fully, just as he is. Become aware if you are sitting in judgment on him and if so, stop it. Reject your own negative thoughts; do not reject others.

As you do this, you will not get caught up in the whirlpool of feelings and will be available to see who the other truly is, and what's really going on. You will be able to hear and see what they are saying, or what they deeply need from you. The person will feel this as well, and often calm down.

Point: When We Feel Truly Listened to and Accepted, We Feel Loved

Practice: Stop Judging Others

Exercise: Who Are You Judging?

Whenever You Notice Yourself Judging Another, Stop It Cold. Go Cold Turkey.

Make a List of Those You Love to Judge. Give It Up, One by One.

Can it be that there is really something wrong with everyone I meet? Is it truly my place to stand apart and judge everybody? Who made me the judge and jury?

Could it really be possible that others aren't completely deserving of my love?

Practice: What I Reject in Others

Describe the kind of people you usually attract in your life. What part of yourself are they expressing?

Who are you having trouble accepting? Can you try accepting them today? See how you feel. See what now happens between you.

Make a list of the main qualities you reject in others.

Could it be something you might not want to face in yourself?

Can you start to accept these qualities in yourself? Even for a few moments?

Can you develop a little compassion about yourself and others?

Or perhaps you might choose to allow these qualities to subside (in which case you will stop attracting those who have them).

"It is as if we change the very course of life itself by changing our attitudes towards it."

Pillar of Love: Love Has Nothing to Do with any Images or Fantasies of How Anybody Should Be.

"Real love never qualifies, never rejects, demands. It replenishes. It is life illumined."

Fantasies are like imaginary flowers dancing in front of our eyes. Unfortunately, while some of these flowers are beautiful, others are simply weeds. Whether they are weeds or beautiful blossoms, they obstruct our true life. They do not provide a clear picture of ourselves or others. And no matter how happy or excited we become, we can take actions based upon delusions that are harmful or off base.

It is important to realize that these fantasies we have of others have nothing to do with what is true, or what is healthy. And because fantasies are unreal, the needs they foster can never be met, but tease and torture us relentlessly.

These fantasies even cause us to reject ourselves when we do not live up to their false images. True satisfaction arises when we see the truth of our lives and how to live it, not when we are playing with fantasies and toys.

Turning Point: Stop Playing with Toys; Find the Real Thing

"When we are little we play with toys.
When we grow up we put our toys away
And want the real thing."

Much of our life is about playing with toys. When we play with toys, often we feel as though our lives had a purpose. Wonderful fantasies usually accompany our play, and these fantasies provide energy and excitement. But as soon as dreams hit the rock of reality, the false thrill vanishes. What happens to our sense of power and aliveness then?

Practice: When Your Toys Break, Don't Grab for New Ones

When our toys are worn out or break in half, we immediately grab for new ones to play with, like a new relationship. If we do not do this, but stay fully awake in that moment, able to tolerate what may feel like loss, emptiness or sorrow, a new understanding arises, one that cannot be broken and that is not dependent upon anything.

Turning Point: "Throw Away All Thoughts of Imaginary Things"

Uchiyama

The Practice of Reality

Notice when you're spending time in fantasy or day-dream. Realize that you are only with imaginary flowers in the sky. Practice guiding your mind into the present moment and noticing what is really here. Smell what you're smelling, taste what you're tasting, feel the ground beneath your feet as you walk.

The practice of reality grounds us in the truth of what's going on, who we are, and what's available right now. This is a wonderful training for living a real life.

Exercise: Give Your Toys Away

Find something that has been a toy for you that you can part with now. Give it away. See what it's like to be without it. What else appears in its place?

Now, do that with another toy when you're ready. Then another. Finally, give them all away, one at a time. Notice how you are feeling, and what your life is without them.

Practice: What and Who Is In Your life? Today, Let It All Be

See who is really here in your life today. They are your precious jewel.

Instead of hoping for something else, or someone else, be with them completely.

What kind of gift are they bringing to you?

What kind of gift do you have for them in return?

Are you looking at them through the eyes of judgment and rejection, or through the eyes of love?

Last summer I was having lunch in an outdoor café with a dear friend who looked down the street and suddenly became alarmed. It seemed as if something frightening was taking place. As I quickly spun around, I saw a homeless man sauntering down the block in a threatening, half mad manner.

"We'd better go inside the restaurant right away," my friend mouthed.

For a moment I agreed, but then paused and decided to practice the Pillars of Love. I looked at him, knowing that his exterior presentation was not who he truly was, and that inside him, and everyone else, the precious jewel was shining.

In my mind, I bowed to him and said, "Thank you for being my teacher in what it means to love. I grant you the right to be who you are."

It seemed as if he paused for a second. Then he continued on to the corner trash can a few feet from where I was sitting. I watched him as he began rummaging around in the garbage.

Oh my goodness, he's hungry, I thought. The fact struck me directly, as I looked down at my plate full of scrambled eggs.

He turned around and looked at me swiftly. I smiled to him and extended my plate. "Would you like something to eat?" I called out.

Startled for a moment he came ambling over, looked down at my plate and shook his head.

"Thanks, but I like my eggs hard boiled," he responded, and we both burst into laughter.

"Okay," I replied as I shrugged my shoulders.

The game was over. I didn't respond to his mask but to who he really was. He couldn't keep up the front any longer.

We chatted for a moment and he moved along. When he stopped at the light at the corner, a woman was standing there with a little child. All of a sudden the child started to run out into the street where a car was coming. Seeing it happen before she did, he jumped out into the street and pulled the child back quickly, taking good care of him. The mother thanked him and both smiled.

Pillar of Love: What We See in Another We Bring Out in Them.

What we see in another we bring out in them. Our very image of them is extending an invitation for them to see themselves and to behave in a certain way. Take charge of how you see others. Take charge of how you see yourself.

Once you see yourself and others through the eyes of love (even with your so-called negative qualities), a magical thing starts to happen. These negative qualities begin to dissolve. Were they only in the eyes of the beholder?

"When we see truly, we will live truly."

Emerson

INTERLUDE

A DIVINE APPOINTMENT

(Relationships as Spiritual Practice)

CHAPTER 4

Relationships as Spiritual Practice
(The Mother Who Cannot Be Wounded)

Usually we think, I'm in charge of my life. I decide who I'll be in a relationship with, where it's going, how long it will last. when it's over. On one level it seems as if we can choose to enter certain relationships and then choose when to let them go. We can choose to buy a train ticket to go on a particular journey. And, once on the train, we can always choose to get off at any stop we like.

But this isn't necessarily so, especially in relationships. Even when things become difficult, we may find ourselves unable to leave, having to endure that situation for a long while. Even when we don't like someone they often keep reappearing in our lives again and again. We cannot escape them even if we want to.

A great deal of the time we cannot stop or alter what's going on in the relationship, no matter how hard we try. We may be happy and hope the relationship lasts forever, and then, suddenly, it may end. Or a troubled relationship will go on and on, no matter how badly we want it to end.

Pillar of Love: We Have a Divine Appointment to Meet and Be with Another.

Many become depressed when things don't work out as they hoped and take this as personal failure. They think they weren't good enough to make the relationship work. But it's not that. No matter how we feel about it, we have a Divine Appointment to meet certain people, to interact with them for a certain length of time, and at a certain, definite point, to part.

Most do not realize that there are important reasons they have met a particular person and are interacting with them. They do not take time to discover the lessons and gifts the relationship is bringing to them. And they do not offer all that they have to give to that person, either. They may choose to withdraw or resent the person, instead. Many declare themselves victims or martyrs in relationships. A dangerous way to think about things. This will only make the interaction more and more painful and prevent one from seeing what is truly needed.

The Stream of Karma

In Zen a Divine Appointment is called our stream of karma. Other traditions may call it destiny. In the Torah it is called Divine Providence, meaning that all of our lives are planned and guided by the hand of God. This does not mean that we are helpless or victims. Sometimes we're very drawn to be in an activity or with a person; other times we want to get away. But despite our wishes and efforts, we have to be right where we are.

Although we may not be able to control or change the events that are happening, we are always in control of our responses to them. We are in charge of the ways we act, the lessons we learn, how much we grow, how strong we become.

When the same painful relationship or situation keeps appearing in your life, a psychologist will call it the Repetition Compulsion. This is where we unconsciously and compulsively repeat the same situation in our lives over and over, draw them to us. The situation is usually a traumatic situation which we are seeking to master now. We are desperate to make the situation turn out differently (which it seldom does). In a sense, this is also a fine description of the Wheel of Karma which keeps turning and draws to us exactly what we need.

According to the Buddha, human life is run by karma, an endless chain of cause and effect, reaching back through time, composed of our thoughts, words and deeds. This karma repeats until it is "purified," until the we have learned from the situation, forgiven it, experienced whatever it is we have done to others. Now, once again in this relationship we are being given an opportunity to balance things out, pay our debt.

In other scriptures we say, *"As we sow, so shall we reap."*

That which we think, say, or do has consequences that extend into time. When certain conditions come together, these karmic seeds, or consequences, ripen. The effects blossom in our lives. Sooner or later, all seeds we have planted yield their fruits, bitter seeds, bitter fruit. Sweet seeds, sweet fruit. The process is continuous.

For example, we may take and take from others. But what do we give in return? How are the scales balanced? Sooner or later we must receive in our lives exactly what we have given.

In Judaism this process is called Tikkun. A Tikkun is a way of balancing the soul for past actions that have to be repaired. When something painful happens, it is beneficial to think of it this way; it takes away our sense of victimhood.

Turning Point: May This Experience Be a Tikkun

We can say, "May this experience be a Tikkun for me," or "May this experience be a balancing for me. May I learn from it and grow."

When we view our painful, seemingly random encounters this way, we are infusing them with meaning, order, and benefit. Rather than becoming angry, lashing out and keeping the cycle going, we are turning the suffering into something positive, a cause for clarity and growth.

For example, there is a teaching in Judaism that when you are insulted, if you do not reply, your sins are wiped away. The important part here is not replying, not lashing back out again, keeping the cycle going.

What's Wrong? I Haven't Been Insulted in Two Weeks

There's a wonderful story of three rabbis who took this deeply to heart. They actually looked forward to being insulted, so they could have their sins (past errors) wiped away and set the slate clean. One day one of the rabbis looked downcast and another asked him why.

The rabbi said, "I don't think God loves me anymore."

"What are you talking about?" the other rabbi, asked, aghast.

"Well," said the first rabbi, "I haven't been insulted in two weeks."

Here the insult had turned into an act of love for the rabbi, rather than a cause for rage.

Rather than be upset, when we learn how to respond with gratitude toward every encounter we have, we can finally fulfill the reason we are meeting, and the relationship can become whole and complete. Then we can receive the gift the other is bringing, see the true reason we've met.

The idea of karma, tikkun, destiny, or past debts that have come to be fulfilled appears in one form or another in all the world's scriptures. This is also the idea of balancing the scales, learning, setting things right. This puts the relationship in a larger perspective, where we can grow, feel love and correct wrongs.

Pillar of Love: Turn Your Relationships into Spiritual Practice.

Turning Point: See All Relationships as Divine Encounters

Even in a very difficult relationship, this perspective will calm you down and turn things around. Rather than fight the person or situation, you pause and ask why this situation is being brought to you.

Ask yourself, **what is needed in this situation to make the relationship complete and whole? Are there past debts that have come to be fulfilled?**

Practice: With Whom Do You Have a Divine Appointment?

Take a few moments to view your relationships as divine encounters. Especially the ones you are having difficulty with. Instead of fighting and resenting it, here are some actions to reveal what's truly needed to make it beneficial for all.

Accept Things Just as They Are.

Stop Fighting the Person.

Say Yes. Give Up Resisting Them.

Let Go of Resisting the Situation

We always say no to what disturbs us and this creates more tension and harm. We think that resisting a person will keep them away, but the opposite is true. Whatever we resist we draw to ourselves and keep everything jammed and in place. The great art of saying yes, of giving up resistance, honors and welcomes the flow of life, actually makes room for change. Here are some steps to let go of resistance. They are actually very easy and pleasant to do. And, although they may be counterintuitive at first, they work powerfully.

Let the Situation Last as Long as It Does

Instead of praying for things to end or do all kinds of things to get out of the relationship, let it last as long as it does. It will anyway. And so much anxiety and negativity will fade away as you surrender to what is happening right now.

Give Up Hoping for Resolution: Let It Turn Out as It does

So much pain in relationships arises because we have a strong picture of how we want things to turn out. We spend enormous time and energy trying to fix people and events. We scold, fight, do whatever we can to change things. None of these work in the long run and these kinds of activities take a great toll upon all. Just give it all up. Let things turn out as they do and see how things start resolving on their own. Honor that, allow it.

Let Go of Wanting to Change the Person

Of course when we are in a painful relationship the first thing we do is jump in to change, control or fix the other person. We want to make the relationship feel good, though we may not have any idea of what the greater good in the situation may be. And, again, the more we struggle to change a person the more they will resist, and the more we are caught in their grip. Most importantly, trying to change another is not loving them. We are rejecting who and what they are right now and they feel it.

When a person feels loved, understood and accepted, you are giving them the space to be who they are at that moment, and it is inevitable that they will then grow and change on their own.

Take time to discover the gift that they are bringing to you.
Each relationship has a gift for you. Find out what it is. See the person as coming bearing gifts, and it will be revealed.

A Great Sacred Friend

"When someone whom I have helped
or in whom I have placed great hope
harms me with great injustice,
may I see that one as a sacred friend."

Shantideva

Pillar of Love: See All as a Great Sacred Friend.
This person is a great, sacred friend because he has come into our lives to teach us patience, endurance, compassion, to purify us of negative karma or poisons that we have accumulated over long periods of time. A painful event would not be now happening to us if we had not sown certain seeds, either through our thoughts, deeds or feelings. Nothing is random or purposeless.

Understanding this, we stand up tall, accept what is happening and take responsibility for our part in how we receive what is going on, how we perceive others, respond, and interact with them. As we do this, it is easy to see that our suffering has its root within our false illusions and actions.

This incredible teaching from the great Buddhist sage Shantideva is addressing the divine appointments we have. When we have been terribly hurt, treated unfairly or terribly disappointed, rather than lashing out in rage or revenge, Shantideva sees that this person has come for a reason, to offer an opportunity to love and to grow. That is why they are not an enemy, but a Great Sacred Friend.

Taking this point of view, and living in this manner, we will find it impossible to feel the depth of hurt we normally would. Instead, we might even feel gratitude. This encounter then has the possibility of opening the doors of our hearts even wider, and helping us see more deeply into the very essence of our lives.

The Mother Who Cannot Be Wounded

Another great sage, the Jillellamudi Mother in India, was pointing to the same truth. When asked who she was she replied, "I am the Mother who cannot be wounded." What an amazing reply. She refused to hold anyone at fault. "Throw flowers or knives at me, it's all the same," she went on.

How could it be all the same? Because the Mother's very core was based upon love. She was here only to give love, and therefore was utterly protected under all circumstances. The Jillellamudi Mother was born in a beautiful and rare state of being. She was the essence of a true mother, with a totally nourishing heart, unable to harm or be harmed.

Most of us live with fear of being hurt or hurting someone. Often a mother will look at their child and say, "Look what you've done to me. You don't make me happy, and now I'm suffering."

Naturally, this creates a lot of guilt, pain, sense of failure and inadequacy. Not only do some mothers do this, but many of us behave this way in our relationships as well. It seems to be part of the human condition, using others to make us happy or meet our needs.

But, Shantideva never sees opponents, he sees great sacred friends. And the Jillellamudi Mother offers a different sense of what is possible. As the Mother who cannot be wounded, she is saying, "I am unconditionally here for you. I grant you the right to be who you are. Who you are does not reflect on me. I am in a state of love, and thus always have all I need. I'm not using you or using this relationship to make me happy. I am already happy. Being filled with love, nothing is missing and nothing can hurt me." As time went on all kinds of people came to see the Mother. When someone came, she just made sure they were fed.

If You Throw Roses or Knives at Me It's All the Same

All kinds of people came to see her, some trying to trip her up. There are those who are addicted to tripping up others, throwing knives at them in all kinds of ways. The Mother's true response to them was, "If you throw roses or knives at me it's all the same."

How could it be all the same? Because she didn't want anything back from anyone. She was only there to give. When you're in that condition, you cannot be wounded because whatever is thrown at you doesn't hit. When you're filled with love, negativity doesn't hit you because you're not resonating with it. You're not looking for praise or approval for anything. You have it all, you are it all. If you're filled with love, what else do you need?

Open Your Own Treasure House

I'm not setting the Jillellamudi Mother up as some kind of an ideal that we should all try to become. It's not about comparing ourselves to her, and naturally falling short. It's always a mistake to compare ourselves to others; we're not here to become someone else. We're here to become ourselves. To open up our own Treasure House. Love expresses itself differently in every person.

An Invitation

The Mother extended an invitation. Not an ego ideal, to compare oneself to, or imitate. It was an invitation to see what one person was capable of, to go within and see that possibility exists within you. In her presence it was easier to get in touch with the love within. People realized it was truly possible to live another way. Vibrations of love go out into the universe, touch, heal and draw those we never see, but who resonate.

Why Am I Wounded?

When we hear of someone like the Mother who cannot be wounded, it makes us wonder, why am I wounded? Or, why do I wound myself?

Addicted to Our Suffering

Unfortunately, some of us are addicted to our suffering. We cling to our anger and memories of how we've been hurt. It's easy to waste an entire life dwelling on that.

Victims of Our Own Misunderstanding

But none of it is true. You're a gift to life, not a victim. You're only a victim of your own misunderstanding. Perhaps you've never known of a different way or alternative. Most have never realized that they could become a huge tree in the garden of life, sheltering all beings, inviting them to open their vistas to a brand new life.

> *"It is as if we change the very
> course of life itself by changing
> our attitudes towards it."*

ENDING THE WAR

"Drinking a cup
Of green tea,
I stopped the war."

CHAPTER 5

Addiction to Battle

Sooner or later most relationships are headed to the battleground. After the initial infatuation and honeymoon, conflict and struggle for power and control often appear. Many realize this and are reluctant to enter a relationship due to fear of the hurt, rejection and loss that may be coming up ahead.

Are Relationships a Game of Destroy or Be Destroyed?

It can be so painful waiting for this loss and rejection to take place that some do things to actually bring it about. They show their worst sides, pick fights, test the other constantly. Anything to get the painful rejection over with fast! It can feel safer to destroy the relationship before it sneaks up from behind and destroys them instead.

But are relationships a game of destroy or be destroyed? Or are they an incredible gateway into the heart of our lives?

Pillar of Love: Our Suffering Is Never Caused by Another, But by the Ways in Which We Respond.

When we suffer in relationships, we assume it's because of what the other person has said or done. Then we spring into action, blame, attack, or try to change the person in some way. Or, feeling like victims, we may simply leave or withdraw our love.

We Are Always in Charge of the Ways in Which We Respond

But the pain *we* are feeling and perpetuating is always caused by *our own responses*. Anger, revenge, guilt, blame and sorrow poison and harm the one who is living with them. We can allow our angry feelings to rule the day or we can choose to respond differently.

The Addiction to Anger

Where does this anger come from? Why are we so quick to attack others, to fall into anxiety and depression? In order to remove the fuel from the wars that erupt in our relationships we must explore our addiction to anger, and the torment it inevitably brings. Why do we cling to our anger so tenaciously and feel it is a source of strength?

Shot by a Poison Arrow

When the Buddha was asked who he was he said he was a physician who had come to cure the ills of the world. He said we'd all been shot with a poison arrow and he'd come to pull the arrow out. He did not come to analyze the length of the arrow or what angle it went in. His teachings were simply showing us ways to pull the arrow straight out. To dissolve negative karma, take ourselves off the merry-go-round.

The Three Poisons

Buddha described the three poisons we were afflicted with as greed, anger and illusion. These poisons cause us to live our lives in a state of confusion, pain and dissatisfaction, where nothing is ever quite right. We're so accustomed to this condition we take it for granted. Grief, upset and constant complaints just seem like a natural part of daily life. And, although we are unaware of them, these poisons manifest in so many ways.

We have so many desires that we cannot fulfill which cause endless frustration and suffering. Some of these desires seem to be so fundamental to our lives, we feel we can't live without them. For example, although everything constantly changes, there is a basic desire to keep everything the same. A yearning for safety and security.

But life arises as it arises. It is our demand that it turn out differently that causes our suffering, and the suffering we inflict upon others. We set up many demands. It is not the outcome of what happens that is so difficult, but that the outcome does not meet our impossible demands.

Impossible Demands

We demand that everyone love us, no matter who. We demand this of people who have no idea of how to love, who do not even approve of themselves. And we also demand this of people we do not approve of or love anyone at all. We demand that life meet our expectations, give us our just due. Of course we have no idea what our just due is, but we demand it anyway.

As we move along in life something's always wrong with the people we meet. No one lives up to our images or expectations. And, as this image of who we are supposed to be is only a fantasy, even when we do fulfill it, the experience never brings deep happiness or fulfillment.

Rather than dwell upon what we give to life, we only dwell upon what we get. Anger arises easily when we feel we're not getting enough, and greed pushes us to use our time getting more and more. However, no matter how much we receive, often the sense of emptiness lingers. And no matter how much we cling to our demands, life moves and changes as it does.

Meet the Monkey Mind

The monkey mind is the voice of the ego, driving us relentlessly. It is the part of ourselves that is constantly restless, chattering, craving, fearing, unable to be satisfied, spoiling whatever is at hand. It judges, rejects, lashes out, and is always completely convinced that it is correct, no one else. Little by little, this monkey mind imprisons us in a cage without bars. Life becomes smaller and tighter, hope dims, confusion increases and finally desperation can arrive.

Then we become frantic and do all we can to get rid of the pain and anger within. Most do this by trying to control external conditions and people. We search for what we like, discard what we don't like, and often go from one relationship to the next to fill the hunger within.

But true gratification will never come that way. Living from desire to desire creates craving and addiction. We become slaves of our desires—the more we satisfy them, the hungrier we can become. At best this is substitute gratification, a counterfeit of the deep peace we are truly longing for.

The Poison of Anger

When we live this way, it's inevitable that anger will fuel most of our days. In our culture, anger is often encouraged and even valued. People are encouraged to express the anger they feel, "assert" themselves in opposition to others, stand up for their rights. When a person becomes able to do this, he is considered to be healthy, not a victim of abuse.

Those who cannot assert themselves are thought to have weak ego structures and poor boundaries. Some are described as *masochists* who enjoy being punished, as a way to relieve unconscious guilt. In this frame of reference anger is seen as an expression of strength, a way to protect a fragile self.

Good Turns to Bad and Bad Turns to Good

Human life is fluid. What can be upsetting and bad one moment turns good the next. Our lives can be described as a process which contains all permutations. As we practice we learn not to leap into anger but to recognize it as a poison along with the danger and pain it contains.

Anger Is Not an Expression of Strength

Anger causes all kinds of destruction; it is one of the three poisons, a great affliction. The rush we get from anger is counterfeit, a substitute for real strength. It is a known fact that anger decreases our health, immune system and ability to respond positively. It provides counterfeit strength, is a bully and functions like a drug.

Anger as Identity

For many anger becomes the basis of their identity. They think I'm tough, I'm strong, I have a right to be angry. This is just anger speaking, twisting and distorting the truth. Others feel that without anger, they would be weak and vulnerable, unable to protect themselves. They'd be a pushover, a doormat, a fool. Naturally, once again, the opposite is *true*. Anger weakens, creates a false sense of power or confidence, which vanishes quickly.

We have no idea of the true strength, confidence, power and meaning that would fill them, as anger is eradicated. This would be a strength that did not arise and vanish, like a high from a drug.

Who Would I Be Without My Anger?

Anger and pain can become familiar, comforting, giving us a sense of being someone important. They can also provide a false rush of energy, which makes us feel as if we're in control.

The deeper truth is that anger keeps us out of control. We cannot think or see correctly when we are taken over. Road rage blinds us. The desire to dominate another or possess them prevents us from ever tasting the fullness we are so hungry for.

Anger also prompts us into the identity of being a victim, with the secondary benefit of controlling others through guilt. Completely encased in our own self-centered interest, we love to see ourselves as the wronged victim. We then blame the other and want them to suffer as we do. Whatever we want for another inevitably comes back at us.

Many have no idea who they truly are and hold fast to conflict and battles simply to feel strong. They feel love that will make them weak, open and vulnerable, at the mercy of whatever happens.

Pillar of Love: My True Strength Is in Openness.

Once again, the opposite is true. The more open we are, the more we act upon the truth of love, the stronger, more centered and real we become and our lives cannot help but flower.

Removing the Fuels for the Angry Mind

There are various fuels the angry mind requires. Without these fuels, our anger will simply flare up and burn out. However, we inadvertently feed the fire continually, then wonder why we are burning inside.

There are many ways to remove the fuels, to let go of the poison of anger. Let's explore them now.

Turning Point: Let Go of Your Addiction to Hatred

Practice: Stop Clinging to Anger

We cling to anger as though it were our best friend. Take note of the ways you hold onto your anger, what you think it will do for you, and what the true result is. A great help in letting go of the poison of anger is seeing the harm it does, that anger is not your friend, has no value for you. Anger is poison, not medicine, and will damage all who cling to it.

When anger arises, see yourself opening your hand and your heart and letting the anger go. You are always senior to your anger. You are always able to say hello to it and then let it drift away.

Communicating During Anger

Practice: Be still. Stay in the Silence and Listen for the Truth.

Before you communicate in a state of anger, stop and feel what is happening within. Experience the feeling. Realize that you are in the midst of an affliction, and that whatever your anger is telling you is not true. It is clouding your mind and vision. You are not seeing the situation fully. For now, let the other person be right. Just listen. Say nothing.

What Is Real, the Rage or the Love?

Later on when you're calmer you'll see things differently. Then you can look closely and see what is real. And you'll be so glad you kept silent.

Ask yourself, what is real here? The rage or the love underneath? Moments of anger come to all of us, one way or another. How do we react then? Do we escalate the violence? Do we give in to hatred? If we can become totally present, quiet and focus on the practices, our new state of being itself will harmonize and change many things. As we see the truth of the matter we have no desire to hold onto the anger, or engage with the lies it tells.

Turning Point: Do Not React, Respond

Practice: Hold Your Seat

Hold your seat is a direction from the Tibetan Buddhist Lojong practice. It advises us to stay steady and still, whatever storm arises. We don't run away or react blindly, but stay centered and open to experiencing what is really going on.

One of the aspects of holding your seat is learning how not to react but to respond. The word *respond* comes from responsible, able to respond. To be awake and available. As we hold our seat, it's easier to respond and stay centered. This is a lifelong practice that inevitably harnesses our energy and creates beneficial responses.

To stay steady and centered during the experience of anger, not to lash out, is the mark of a ripened man.

Welcoming Our Shadow

The more we hide from, ignore or repress our anger and project it onto others, the more power these qualities have over us. And the greater likelihood they will appear in our lives as hurt, illness, rejection or repetitive situations which we feel we have no control over.

Robert Bly calls this the shadow aspect of human life. He says that we all throw unacceptable parts of ourselves into our unconscious, hide from it and let it fester there. Then we see these qualities in individuals and situations around us.

Turning Point: Eat Your Shadow

Eating our shadow is the act of reclaiming and experiencing these hidden feelings and qualities. We do not project them onto others, but realize they are part of us and welcome them into awareness. The very act of welcoming all feelings and accepting difficult qualities takes the steam out of them.

Turning Point: It Is Our Resistance to Anger That Gives It Power

The less we resist and oppose feelings, the more readily they dissolve. It is our resistance to them that fuels them and gives them power. When the resistance subsides, they have no strength to remain on their own.

Dissolve False Needs and Wishes

As we dissolves false needs and wishes, we can see what our true needs are, and how to meet them easily. It is the nature of life to provide for real needs. Of course when this happens, the angry mind has no place to stand.

Make a list of your needs and wishes. Let go of false needs and harmful wishes. When they arise, don't reach for them again. Just see them for what they are—part of the poison that is harming your life.

The Monk on the Mountain

A monk sat in zazen on a mountain for many years. He attained a state of *samadhi* (oneness) and felt deep peace and equanimity. After a time he went down from the mountain back to the city, where the true test of his practice came. As soon as someone spoke to him rudely, anger and pride flared inside of him. "How dare they treat someone like me that way?" he exclaimed.

Does this mean that his time on the mountain was useless? No. It simply means that the roots of anger can go deep. What the monk found inside him back on the streets of the city, the test of his real practice began. And his lessons in moving along.

> *"Sometimes we receive the power to say Yes to Life*
> *Then peace enters us and makes us whole."*
>
> *Emerson*

CHAPTER 6

Healing the Divided Heart

*"All conflicts with others
Are always conflicts within the self."*

Taisen Deshimaru

Conflicts in Relationships

Conflicts in our relationships always mirror the conflicts going on within. Although there's always a part inside longing for love and connection, another part may crave distance or enjoy power struggles. That part wants to be on top, to win, to conquer, to be in charge.

The part engaged in opposition and resistance can be called ego, the part of us that is only concerned with its own needs, wants and beliefs. The ego's concern is how will things work out for *me?* What will *I* get out of this? It doesn't want to become too close or intimate for fear it will lose its self-absorption and disappear.

Ego fears that love will destroy it and will fight love in all its forms. It overwhelms us with myths and mirages to keep us distracted and entertained.

Clinging to Our Suffering

Pillar of Love: Ego Is the Enemy, Not Anyone Else.

When we cling to our suffering we are clinging to ego. We do not realize that is the enemy, not anyone else. The ego is always in opposition to others and to our higher interests as well. All of the practices in this book are designed to undo the ego's hold upon our lives.

The ego thrives upon war and conflict as it builds up its false sense of importance. Then the ego can prove it is bigger and better than you. And of course, ego must always be right!

All loneliness and struggle arise from the myths and mirages the ego presents. Let's explore these myths, so we can expose their falsity and head in a new direction.

The Foundation of Ego-Based Relationships
Who's Smart? Who's Dumb?
Who Needs the Other More?
What Can I Reject About Them?
I'm Right, They're Wrong!
They're Not Good Enough
All My Pain Is Their Fault

Each of these ways of being can be easily exposed and undone by a Pillar of Love!

Pillar of Love: When Others Are Wrong I Am Wrong.

"When others are wrong, I am wrong" undermines the ego. It is saying that I am wrong for viewing others as wrong.

Also, as I am always one with others, if they are wrong, I must correct the error in myself as well.

Turning Point: Do Not Praise Yourself and Blame Others

A wonderful step in undermining ego-based relationships is not to praise myself and blame others. This is the heart of all scriptures and this phrase comes from the world of Zen. I do not lift myself and put others down. All negativity projected upon others is clearly seen to simply be negativity in my own mind. We project upon the world what is going on within. Better to take the projections back, to see where these images come from.

Practice: Allow the Other to Be Right

If we allow the other to be right, the fight will end immediately. And we will stay steady and centered during an onrush of anger, which is the mark of a ripened man.

This does not mean to let go of your standards or continue a relationship that may be toxic for you. It means that in the moment, you are making room for the other to be who they are. You're not judging or rejecting. You're giving the other space to be. You also are not projecting your feelings upon them, or wanting them to be different than they are.

At the moment they are who they are. Be with that; do not resist the reality. The more you can accept the moment, who they are right now, the more you are giving them room to grow and change on their own.

Practice: In the Midst of Conflict And Battle, Stop and Allow the Other to Be Right.

Because they are right does not mean that you are wrong. Allow both of you to be right. Or allow yourself to be right later. Take this opportunity to learn about their experience, and honor that.

Turning Point: A Relationship Isn't About Winning or Losing

Practice: Remember What Your Relationships Are Dedicated To.

Say in your mind: I Grant You the Right To Be Who You Are!

You Are My Teacher in What It Means to Love.

The Divided Heart

Much of our lives are lived split between good and bad, love and hate, win and lose. We accept some people and experiences and cling to them, and block out or deny the rest. When we live this way, conflict is inevitable. And how can we be free of the poison of the anger which arises when we aren't able to hold onto what we want? In this way we always live our lives on the lookout for what we don't like and fight it. Somehow we don't see that each of us contains everything, all possibilities.

Turning Point: We Contain Everything

To live in conflict with ourself and others ultimately kills all relationships, because it causes us to look at life through a jaundiced eye. There is inherently something we must guard against and reject. Before we even get to know someone, we push them away.

"Open your hands, if you want to be held."

Rumi

When we open our arms and our heart to the whole world and are willing to meet it just as it is, the whole world opens its whole arms to us as well.

Turning Point: Make Friends With All That Is

The experience of acceptance and oneness is a basic fruit of the principles of this program. We see that the pain we feel so often comes from rejecting and fighting unwanted parts of ourselves, within and without. As we stop fighting and rejecting, an amazing thing happens; no matter who or what comes into our lives, we become able to greet them.

Rather than focus upon the ways in which we are divided, we experience the ways in which we are One. As we make acquaintance with all that is within us, like it or not, we can no longer be at war with others. We see that we contain everything and are all one. And, as we have more compassion for others, our compassion for ourselves grows as well. And we become a friend to all life, rather than an enemy.

Practice: The Turnaround Procedure

This simple and beautiful exercise ends conflict quickly and allows us to reach mutual understanding with ease. The individuals in conflict should write a little scene out which depicts the essence of the problem they're having. Now each should take the role of their opponent and act the scene out for others to see. They must not play their own part, but see and play the situation out through the eyes of their adversary. Before very long their understanding will grow wider. Their fixed point of view and position is broken through. They cannot help but understand fully what the other is going through. New solutions arise in this process quickly. It is fun to do and will be surprising to you.

This is a wonderful practice for reducing pride and separation and allowing us to experience the feelings of another person and develop compassion and oneness.

Reversing Roles: The Turnaround Procedure

Think of someone you are having difficulty with.

Think of a scene that usually happens between you.

Now you are going to act the scene out again. It is helpful to have someone to play the scene with. (If not, do it in your mind.)

To begin, you play the role of the person you are having difficulty with. Become them.

Say what they usually say, do what they do. See how they are feeling. What are they truly needing and wanting from you?

Take a moment to absorb the experience, to really see the interaction from their point of view.

Now we will play the scene out again. This time take your own role. See how differently you see the situation now.

How are you feeling? Say what you feel now, do what you would now like to do.

It's very difficult to feel anger, pride or arrogance once you do this exercise fully. When you actually walk in another's shoes, become them, it's easy to see what they truly want, how they're feeling and the ways in which we are all united.

"Real love never qualifies, never rejects, demands. It replenishes. It is life illumined."

Practice: "Face Each Other and Smile"

Here is a wonderful exercise created by Thich Nat Hanh, the great Zen master involved with engaged Buddhism. When disharmony exists in the Sangha among the body of monks and nuns, this is what he does to dispel it. Naturally this exercise can be applied to any group of individuals.

A) All sit facing another quietly and smile. This smile represents their willingness to be friendly to one another. Before anything at all can be done, there must be mutual willingness to help, not fight. Basic intention is primary.

B) The individuals in conflict know everyone expects them to make peace. No one listens to stories spread by others, or spreads news of the conflicting monks.

C) *Remembrance* – Each person remembers the entire history of the conflict, every detail. All sit patiently and listen to each as they take their turn. In this way *all* thoughts and feelings are included, from both sides of the conflict.

D) *Non-stubbornness* – All expect peace and do their best to create an atmosphere for it. Atmosphere of the assembly is crucial.

E) *Covering Mud with Straw* – A senior monk is appointed to each side of the conflict. Each says something to the assembly to *de-escalate the conflict.* Whatever they say is respected. They speak to cause the others to understand their monk more fully. In this case hard feelings are dissipated. Mud is the conflict, straw is lovingkindness.

F) *Voluntary Confession* – Each monk reveals his own shortcomings and apologizes.

G) *Sacrifice* – All are reminded that the welfare of the entire community is most important. Each monk must make a sacrifice and be ready to accept the verdict.

H) *Accepting Verdict* – The decision is made and each monk must do various things to repair what has happened. Community must accept it. Harmony is thus restored.

This beautiful process is a fine description of Zen practice in action. It includes great respect for all parties concerned, no blame, hatred or harsh judgment, but a fair and deep hearing of all aspects of the situation. The emphasis is not upon who is right and who is wrong. Instead, the emphasis is upon how harmony will be restored. The expectation and desire of all is for harmony, not retribution.

Each party to the conflict takes responsibility for their own part in it, publicly acknowledging their shortcomings and apologizing. In this manner no one is put to shame, both take part together, and forgiveness and compassion are the order of the day. The conflict becomes a great teaching where one has the opportunity to learn, grow, share with others, and dissolve false righteousness and pride.

Fundamentally There Is Not One Thing Wrong with Any of Us

Judging, discarding and clinging cause us to live with a sense of lack. We live frozen with a fear of loss, in a world which is abundant, filled with experiences, relationships and possibilities. And, living this way, it becomes impossible to see that there is not one thing wrong with any of us. We are already full and complete. We must just learn to let go, make room for whatever comes, and allow what has to go, to go.

Now You Are Drinking Your Cup of Green Tea

"Drinking a cup of
green tea,
I stopped the war."

What is this green tea? How can we learn how to drink it? In order to really drink a cup of green tea, to stop the war within and without, we must first become receptive.

As we truly drink the tea we turn our attention to what is here in our life this moment, appreciating it fully. We must deeply appreciate the cup it is served in, and the efforts of those who bring it to us. And we must be fully willing to taste of the tea, take our time and drink it slowly. We cannot just gulp it down.

Sip by sip we receive it, just as we receive our life. We honor the green tea and it honors us. We do this not only with the tea, but with everyone who comes into our life. This is the way the delicious green tea can stop the war that rages within us. It is a shocking moment when we realize that we are all one, subject to exactly the same longings and pressures, brothers and sisters, living briefly on this earth.

"Apples given and oranges received in return."

CHAPTER 7

Empty Your Cup
(Letting Go)

"When They Come We Welcome
When They Go
We Do Not Pursue."

The Great Art of Letting Go

One of the clearest paths to unshakeable love is the great art of letting go. Although letting go is simple and natural, we fight it to the core. We want things to stay the same forever, while life is nothing but change. We fight to hold onto old beliefs and memories, although everything passes and alters every day. Our sense of safety is constantly threatened, as we do not know where true security lies.

When Change Comes

When change comes, our usual reaction is to grab and hold on to what we've had even tighter. We stiffen up, fight and oppose the flow of events. However, the harder we hold, the more we crush what we have in the palm of our hands.

Pillar of Love: The Pain of Change Is Resistance to What Is Happening Right Now.

By holding on, we seek to gain control. We refuse what's happening, run from it, use all our energy to change things. This is the will asserting itself, demanding that life meet our particular demands, pronouncing "I am in charge." But the wind knows better. When it's time to blow, the wind blows. When it's time to be still, there is no flutter. No problem.

However we resist, and the more we resist, the more we crush whatever we have in the palm of our hands. Our resistance gives energy to the experience as well, keeping it stuck to us, engaged in battle.

Holding Onto Everything

We come into life empty-handed and then try to grab and hold onto everything. Immediately, we make claim for ownership. *"This is my mother. She can't go away."*

We want everything and we want it immediately. We want to receive, to hold and possess, forever. Why do we attach and cling so tenaciously? This kind of response seems so automatic and fundamental that we do not question it at all. Yet, in truth, what really belongs to us? What will stay with us forever? Even our bodies have a life of their own.

Most become very proud of what they have accumulated, and believe it is who we are. Soon they are so full they can hardly move, and yet still search for more. Before long every corner of their lives is crammed full and yet they feel empty within.

Attachment is usual, but not natural. Certainly, it is not necessary. It arises out of a deep confusion about who we truly are, what we have and what is happening now. Attachment arises out of a misunderstanding about the nature of our relationships and the fear of being abandoned.

The Gripping Itself Creates the Fear

We feel the tighter we hold on, the less frightened we will be. The opposite is true. The gripping itself creates the fear. We do not yet see that we can never be abandoned. This sense of crushing and being crushed is at the very core of the pain we experience. It is our resistance to the flow of life.

Change Is Not Loss, Just Change

The moment something changes we blame ourselves, feel like failures and grasp on tighter. But life itself is nothing but change. We do not have to experience it as loss, if we are fully aware of this. The more we let go into the flow of life, the more alive we become—and the more we enjoy the new possibilities that are always right in front of our eyes. Try it and see.

Refusing to Allow Change to Happen: The Clinging Mind

Instead of allowing change, we grab and cling for dear life. We are often unaware of and unavailable for what's happening now as we're so occupied holding onto what has already gone.

Along with fear of loss there always comes clinging to what we've accumulated. We hold onto what's unnecessary, terrified of letting go, fearing we'll be empty. The clinging mind never has enough of clinging. It's not only loss that it fights, it opposes reality of all kinds, as it stays stuck in the past. But the more we cling, the more we suffer.

It Is the Clinging Itself That Spoils Your Time Together

See that whatever comes will have to go. Enjoy it while it is here, but don't cling to it tenaciously. It's the clinging that causes pain and spoils the time you have together.

Understanding Attachment

Why do we attach and cling so tenaciously? Attachment is usual, but not natural. Certainly, it is not necessary. It arises out of our deep confusion about who we are, the nature of our lives itself, and where we are ultimately headed. It arises out of a misunderstanding about the nature of relationships and a false fear of being abandoned. We do not take time to know, meet and accept the fundamental nature of the world itself.

Practice: What Do You Cling To?

Make a list of those things in your life you are greatly attached to. Stop and look it over, see what purposes they serve for you. What would happen if you let go of one of them?

Each day this week, let go of one, just for the day. See how loving it feels, how freeing for both of you.

"Gain and Loss, Away with Them, Once and for All."

Sosan

When we view life instead as a process of gain and loss, we will never feel complete or at ease. It is natural for many things to come to us, and then also to go. As we stop constantly trying to gain something and hold onto it, a new life opens. Naturally, this is true of our relationships as well.

What Do We Have That We Can Lose?

When Dogen, a great Zen master of old, returned to Japan after many years of studying Zen in China, the people asked what he brought with him. His reply is famous.

He said, "I've returned with nothing but empty hands."

The Wisdom of Empty Hands

What are these empty hands? Where can we find them? What value are they for us today?

Usually our own hands are full, filled with tasks, problems and possessions that seem impossible to put down. We live our lives holding on tightly to our ideas, possessions, plans and dreams. Then the winds of change come, blow us around and scatter our dreams on the shore. Most go wild trying to pick up the pieces and we hold onto whatever we have.

When change, loss and disturbance came to Dogen he planted himself in the center of the storm, sat unmoving with an open heart and empty hands. He allowed whatever came to come, and whatever left to go. Once Dogen's hands were emptied, they were flexible and useful. And, as he was not clinging to anything, nothing was lost, and the whole world belonged to him. His empty hands also allowed him to be entirely available and free.

The Value of Empty Space

"To See the True Beauty of a Room, Take Everything Out"

A great Zen master, Soen Nakagawa Roshi, offered a different point of view. He said usually when we want to make a room beautiful, we add more and more to it, furniture, paintings, decorations. But to see the true beauty of a room, it is far better to take everything out. Once the room is empty, you can truly see its natural beauty.

Its natural beauty is uncontrived, cannot be tampered with or lost in any way. Just like the empty room, we too must find our natural beauty and open space.

Turning Point: Empty Your Cup

A student sought out a great Zen master to discover the secrets of this universe and what his life truly meant. He traveled far and wide and finally located a Master living simply in a hut on top of a mountain. The student made his way to the hut and the Master welcomed him in. The hut was furnished sparsely and immaculately. The

Master motioned for him to sit down on a mat on the floor and went to boil water for tea. The student waited for the tea to be ready.

The water boiled slowly. The student grew restless, eager to get the preliminaries over with, ask his question and get his answer. He hadn't come for tea, he'd come for an answer. He thought he would get it just like that. He thought the answer was something someone else could give him.

The more restless the student grew, the more slowly the water boiled. Not only was it clear that the student had not acquired patience, it was also clear, as he waited, that he was not at home with himself. He thought some answer presented by another was going to put him at rest.

Finally the tea was ready. The Master gave the student a teacup and the student trembled excitedly.

The Master began to pour the tea, up to the very top of the cup. Even though the cup was filled to the brim, the Master kept on pouring, so that very soon the hot tea spilled over the edges and onto the student's trembling hands.

"What are you doing?" the student cried out.

"What are *you* doing?" the Master replied. "Just like this tea cup you are full of yourself, full of opinions, desires, questions, imagination. How can you receive anything from me when your cup is so full? In order to receive anything, first you must empty your cup."

In order to receive the truth we must be willing to let go of our vain imaginings, become able to taste and appreciate a simple cup of tea. We do not sit before the Master trembling, thinking he has some kind of answer that will make our lives all right. Little by little we begin to realize that our own cup of tea is itself complete.

As we empty our cup we also empty ourselves of ego, demands and self-importance. We become available to see and honor whoever is before us.

Turning Point: Empty Your Cup

As we let go of our endless attachments and accumulations, everything seems precious, no matter what. We want to hold onto it for old times' sake. But it may not be so easy to clean out the drawers. We have not yet learned the value of empty space or how to stop and ask, "Do I need this anymore?" We can just say, "Thank you. This suffices. It is enough."

Practice: Thank You, This Suffices

Thank you and This Suffices are the perfect medicine for all suffering. This Suffices is from a Tibetan Buddhist teaching offered by Tulku Thondup. They are profound and simple solutions to our endless attachments and cravings, and are readily available to all.

When frustration and grasping arise, ask, *What am I wanting now? What is wrong with what I have?* Be completely where you are at this moment, and with what you presently have. We rarely experience what is before us now, as we start wanting something more or better, something which will make our lives seem worthwhile.

A) Whatever is given to you, look at it and say, *"Thank you, this suffices."*

B) Stop and notice what you already have. In what ways are your hands and life overflowing? Rather than focus upon what you're lacking, dwell upon all that is here right now.

This is a practice of dissolving attachment and welcoming all that life offers. Another way of saying this is, *"Thy Will Be Done."*

When we are thankful our hearts are filled and are hands stop grasping. We are not grabbing for more, or clutching onto what we have. Our hands and teacup become empty, flexible and useful. They are open, available, can reach out and touch another, offer comfort and love. They can give and receive, do what is needed when the moment appears. Empty hands are just simply there, like the poppy blowing in the wind.

> *"Just simply alive,*
> *Both of us,*
> *I am the poppy."*

The poppy is alive and blowing in the wind; it is free to enjoy everything. The more we empty our hands, the freer and happier we are as well.

A Bubble, Dewdrop, Flash of Lightning

> *"Thus shall ye think of all this fleeting world:*
> *A star at dawn, a dewdrop, a bubble in a stream;*
> *A flash of lightning in a summer cloud,*

A flickering lamp, a phantom, and a dream."

Diamond Sutra

No one wants to be a dewdrop, a bubble or a flash of lightning. We want to be the center of the Universe. And, in fact, we are, though not in the way we imagine.

This beautiful quote from the Diamond Sutra is a powerful instruction and practice for all. It speaks to the fact of transience, that we are here for a long moment and then gone. This perspective allows us to cherish the moments we have together, and also helps not becoming embroiled with negativity. Most important of all, it reminds us over and over not to cling to what comes, because inevitably, it must go.

Turning Point: "Dwelling as Change Brings Peace"

Accepting and living with impermanence is a great remedy for suffering. When we realize that life and people will not be here with us forever, we can see them more clearly and appreciate them so much more vividly. We can also stop the process of accepting, rejecting and clinging, which causes all so much pain.

Pillar of Love: Let Everything Come and Then Go.

Practice: Watch the ever changing seasons, years, moments, thoughts, moods and feelings that arise and depart. Just watch them. Let them come and let them go. Do the same with your relationships. See people enter your life, stay for a season (or many seasons) and then inevitably depart. See the nature of life itself as a constant process of change. Familiarize yourself with this process, accept this natural flow, and you and your relationships will be in harmony. A well-known Zen saying is:

"When They Come We Welcome, When They Go, We Do Not Pursue."

Welcome whatever and whoever comes into your life, and then let them go when it is time to depart. Try this with all that comes to you in life, including your relationships. It is the heart of kindness not to cling to others. Become at home with change. It is lack of knowing who we truly are, the nature of the universe and our real place in it that causes us to hold on so tight. As we empty our hands and live in harmony with the deep truths of life, we are filled continually.

"A traveler, let me be known thus,
This autumn evening."

CHAPTER 8

The Fine Art of Parting
(Becoming Complete)

"A traveler
Let me be known thus,
This autumn evening."

In the absolute sense, there is no parting. Yet we meet, touch and have to go. We then suffer so much, feeling that our loved ones are leaving and that we are ultimately alone. Deep chords of abandonment can resonate within.

When this happens, we become grievous and sad. Sometimes grief is so overpowering that it is difficult to move on and love again. When it comes time to say good-bye, we may see only that which we are losing. We may not yet be able to see that which neither comes nor goes.

"Who Is the Host, Who Is the Guest?"
Guests come to visit, the host remains at home. The guest is a temporary visitor, the host receives whomever comes. While the host receives many visitors, he or she neither comes nor goes. In our relationships at different

times we play the role of both host and guest. At certain times we become part of the passing world, appear as a guest in someone else's life. We wander here and there, enjoy the scenery, come and go.

When we participate in life as the host; even if we are traveling, we are always at home. When centered within our inner home, changing guests and events are all welcomed. We realize that all is passing, so we do not cling or demand that others stay longer than they can.

Turning Point: When Parting Remember All That You Have Received

Some fear loss so deeply that it prevents them from being close while they are with the ones they love. Others cannot bear to be open and vulnerable, knowing that someday the relationship will have to end. Closeness seems like the greatest danger.

There are so many walls we erect for protection. But, living our lives behind these walls, we grow lonely and sad. Parting, when it does come then, hits us even harder then. We missed the chance for closeness we had.

Pillar of Love: Stop Holding Back: Be Together Without Reservation.

Andrew, deep in the throes of loss, described his regret eloquently. "I was always afraid of my father, afraid to know who he really was. I was afraid to share my true feelings with him and let him know how much I cared. Then, one day, he was gone and I suddenly began to feel all the love for him I never expressed."

This is an experience that many go through. Perhaps it's safer to feel and express our love when the person isn't there. It can be easier to love a memory than a real person in the flesh and blood.

However, if we can dare to really love a person completely, use our time together fully, it's much easier when we must part. If we cannot, the dread of parting always hangs between us, the echo of all that has been unsaid and undone.

> *"It's not loss itself that is so painful, it's the unlived life."*

Most of the time we're stuck in the middle, holding onto the person, yet holding back many things we feel and want to say. When we learn to be together without reservation, parting becomes much more natural. We are complete. It's when we hold back, have not lived out our time together, that we cannot bear to let someone go.

Completing Our Relationships

In order to really say good-bye, we have to feel complete with the other. This means we have to feel as if we have done, said and experienced all that was there for us to do, say, give and receive with the other person.

Part of becoming complete is to allow the other person to truly know us, and to truly know them in return. Then the relationship has been fulfilled. We have given the gifts we have for them, and received what they had for us. We've been true. Although we will miss the person, they have become part of us now; something vital has been integrated.

At first it may seem too frightening or overwhelming to complete a relationship. It can be hard to know where to begin, or how the other may react. Also, you may feel that no matter what you say or do, it won't really change anything. It's too late.

However, it's never too late to complete a relationship. Even one moment of being present and truthful begins to dissolve much pain of the past. At every moment we have the opportunity to be the person we truly are. (And we can also complete relationships even after the person has passed away.)

At Any Moment We Can Be the Person We Want to Be

It doesn't matter if the other person does or does not wish to share their feelings with you. Your own act of truthfulness releases you from a sense of incompletion, no matter how they react. You have done what had to be done. You will feel different regardless of how they respond. And, in some subtle way, they will too.

Where to Begin

Begin simply by telling the other person what they have meant to you, what they gave you in your life. Find the good things and discuss the problems. It never helps to pretend that negative thoughts and feelings don't exist. The way you express them makes the difference.

This is not time for harsh words or blame. When negative feelings and experiences are calmly brought to the surface without blaming the other for them, but taking responsibility for your own feelings and responses, room is made available for love to emerge.

For example, you might say, "I felt hurt by something that happened, but it's over now. I learned a great deal from it." This kind of communication will remove an enormous weight and burden from both of you.

Turning Point: The Power of Acknowledgment

Acknowledgment is an incredibly powerful action. Most of the time we acknowledge what didn't work in our relationships, bring it up again and again. It's less common to take time to acknowledge to the other what did work, the beautiful moments, how their words or action uplifted and supported you. Many of us have no sense of how we're impacting others, the good we may have done. By simply acknowledging who the person is for you, or what their simple action means or meant to you, not only do doors open between you, but you feel complete.

Practice: Acknowledge the Other for Who They Are to You

This is a wonderful practice that can be done routinely, all through a relationship. We somehow think others know how we feel about them and the impact of their deeds and behavior. They do not. Most have no idea. It is an incredible gift to let others know how their actions have touched you. This in and of itself creates a wonderful bridge between you. It is a true source of inspiration and encouragement.

The very act of acknowledgment is an act of love and appreciation. It is impossible not to be moved when someone is sharing their truth, impossible not to feel loved. Practice this on an ongoing basis. Simply let others know what their deeds and words mean to you. Doing this on an ongoing basis really makes a relationship feel complete, day by day.

Acknowledge Yourself as Well

Acknowledge yourself as well. There is so much we do all day long that seems to drift off somewhere, never to be noticed or received. The practice of acknowledgment works wonderfully when you do it with yourself as well.

Keep a small journal and write down moments to acknowledge yourself for. So often we do or say things that are meaningful, that we allow to just drift away. Perhaps you might acknowledge a difficult step you took, perhaps it's a deed you really respect. This is a way of mirroring back to yourself who you are, and what is fulfilling.

Turning Point: Communicate Honestly with Love

When we haven't been able to speak truthfully or to listen, this is often experienced as a kind of withdrawal. This withdrawal itself contributes so much to the pain and loneliness we feel, and to the difficulty of becoming complete. We think we are protecting each other by pretending and playing games, but the loneliness this creates is the worst pain of all. When we are real with ourselves and one another, the moment and the relationship are always fulfilled.

Practice: Becoming Complete

The following guided meditation will guide us in becoming complete with another. It is very effective. As you do it, old feelings of sadness, failure or anger may emerge. Do not be afraid of them. Let them emerge and let them go.

Close your eyes, relax, become comfortable. Imagine yourself in a very beautiful place where you feel safe, at home and comfortable in.

Now, picture someone you love whom you are incomplete with. Bring him/her to you now. Think back over your time together. Let pictures and memories come to you.

What do you want to say to him/her? Can you say it now? Let him/her answer you now. What does the person want to reply?

What is the most beautiful thing you remember between you? Tell him/her. What is it that you would like to change?

What are you still wanting from this person? What is there left for you to do?

Take a moment now and realize that the person is about to leave you. What needs to happen between both of you in order for you to feel peaceful and complete?

What has to happen in order for you to be able to let him/her go? Can you let it happen? (If not, can you talk about it with him/her?)

Is there something you want the person to do or say to you in order for you to be able to let him/her go? Ask the person to say it to you.

Now, picture the person leaving. Picture yourself letting him/her go. How do you feel now? What has he/she left with you? What has he/she taken away?

Pillar of Love: Forgiveness Completes and Heals the One Who Offers It.

Underneath all of our misdeeds and pain, there is always love and forgiveness waiting. It may not seem that way momentarily, but it is so. As soon as we have forgiven a person and received their forgiveness in return, all is settled and complete. Only the love between us remains.

If we do not experience completion and forgiveness, we may spend years occupied in grief or bitterness after a person has gone. We are then simply holding on to anger, holding on to the person in a negative way.

Practice: The Forgiveness Process

You can do this practice in person, and also in your mind. If the person is not alive, or here in person, it can be equally effective.

Ask for forgiveness for whatever it is that you think you did to hurt this person. Offer him/her your forgiveness in return for whatever he/she may have done to hurt you.

In a case where it seems difficult to give or receive forgiveness the following is helpful:

List all of the lovely things the person ever did for you.

Make a conscious effort to find goodness in the person.

The goodness is there, and if you cannot find it, the block exists in you, not in the other one.

Now, also find your own beauty and goodness. Make a list of all the lovely things you did for the person.

Tell the other person how happy and proud you are of him/her and of yourself. Congratulate each other.

It is often so much easier to find fault and to hate and blame ourselves and each other. It is easy to forget or gloss over the fine things about each other and ourselves.

This can be reversed consciously. Dwell upon the ways in which you helped, loved, and cheered the other person.

What wonderful things can you do for him/her now? Are you willing to do them?

If not, why not? (Does it feel better to stay locked up in revenge?)

When we are open and truthful with someone it is so much easier to let them go. And, although the other person may take his leave of us, the love stays with us and helps us to grow and move on.

It may be said that most of our lives we are holding back, waiting for the perfect moment to forgive.

Look and see what you want from the person, before you can offer forgiveness.

Whether or not you receive it, the real gift to yourself is just to forgive anyway.

Every moment is the perfect moment to offer forgiveness. It's simply a matter of whether or not we are willing to open and love.

> *"Before you try to straighten another,*
> *Do a harder thing,*
> *Straighten yourself."*

SECTION THREE

GIVING AND RECEIVING

"Apples given
And oranges received
In return."

CHAPTER 9

The Gift of Giving

"True giving is its own reward."

The Zen Master and the Robber

An elderly Zen master was living in a small hut on a mountain which was simple and bare except for the few possessions he needed. One night a robber broke into his hut and took everything in it, including the clothes the Zen master wore on his back.

After the thief left, the Zen master looked through the window at the moon that was shining in. He sighed and said, "Too bad I can't give him this beautiful moon, too."

Nothing the Zen Master Had Could Be Taken Away

This robber could not rob the Zen master because the Zen master only wanted to give whatever he had. There was nothing the Zen master had that could be taken away. He was deeply fulfilled by each moment of his life and his desire to hold on and accumulate was gone. Of course, given his condition, he had no need to reject or hate the robber. He had only compassion for him.

Only Wanting to Give

Much suffering arises from our experience of loss. The suffering includes distrust of others, fearing they will take what we have and run away. Many become reluctant to give due to this. Stinginess of heart develops, constricting all aspects of their lives. Some will give only if they can get something in return. Or they give reluctantly with constant suspiciousness, imputing bad motives to all.

But the Zen master only wanted to give the robber this beautiful moon. He wanted to give him a way to taste the fullness and beauty of life. When we only wanted to give, bear no grudges and are not grasping at what we have, our hands and heart become wide open. Not only can we give, but we are able to receive what life is offering.

What a wonderful way to live and to be in relationship with life. But first we must understand what true giving and receiving are.

Counterfeit Giving

When you give to get something in return this is not true giving. It is barter, like being in the marketplace. Often we give to hold onto others, or to feel good about ourselves. Sometimes we give gifts that are too costly for us and resent the gift later on. This balance between true giving and receiving is vital for a healthy relationship.

Turning Point: Don't Give to Get

Some give from a sense of debt, feel they must give to another constantly even when they are drained or receiving nothing in return. This too is not true giving. True giving fills a person. That kind of giving is itself the reward.

Some feel they are useless and empty, with nothing to offer anymore. A deep sense of shame can pervade their lives. For these individuals, especially, it is necessary to give whatever they can, a smile, a drawing, a word of encouragement.

The very act of giving and receiving freely opens our hands up and helps to let go. But few give freely. There can be many hidden intentions when giving, to hold onto someone, to flatter, cajole, make them dependent. Some give expecting a big return on their gift. They give with the feeling that the person is now indebted to them. This is not true giving, just a way to assert their own power and control.

The more we give, the more we realize we have. The best way to stop feeling deprived and empty is to open up and give what you have, a smile, a word of encouragement, a letter, a song, some food.

Pillar of Love: A Relationship Is Not Merchandise to Be Bought or Sold.

But a true relationship is not merchandise to be bought or sold. A true relationship is based upon real giving without wanting or expecting anything in returned.

"Return Home,

Purify Your heart
Ask Nothing For Yourself."

Pillar of Love: Giving Without Wanting Anything in Return Brings Joy.

Turning Point: True Giving Is Its Own Reward

This kind of giving is called *Mushotoku* in Japan. You just give, without focusing on the consequences of giving, or on wanting anything in return. The joy and fulfillment comes from the act of giving itself. This state of being is freeing and joyful. You are not demanding any particular outcome, just making an offering with a full, sincere heart. That is true giving, and the person who receives the gift is freed by it as well. Along with giving to them we are freeing them from any debt to us, or having to do or give anything in return.

The pain and anguish we feel in giving comes from our inner demand for something in return.

Turning Point: Stop Wanting to Get Anything in Your Relationships

Mushotoku

Practice: What Do You Want from Your Relationships?

Take a good look at what you really want from your relationships.

Dwell with this question, write it down.

Most of the time it is unlikely that we will receive just what we've wanted. And by insisting upon it, we have rooted our happiness in the way another responds. Now we are dependent upon their circumstances, needs and moods. But it is easy to turn all this around, and for both of you to be delighted.

Turning Point: Give the Other All They Want

Give others what they want. This may sound either foolishly simple, or revolutionary. However you think of it, it's a powerful act. Usually we decide if someone really needs something, if they deserve it, if we can manage to give it. But ultimate generosity is ultimate joy. Just say yes.

Give them whatever they want, without expecting anything back in return. Don't secretly demand that they even appreciate your gift, or that it makes them happy. Let them feel as they do. Demanding that your gift makes them happy is creating a reward for you.

Takahatsu

The practice of takahatsu in Japan demonstrates this kind of giving and receiving beautifully. Takahatsu, or begging, is an ancient spiritual practice for monks and nuns. In all kinds of weather, monks walk one behind another into town, in sandals or barefoot, wearing large straw hats with their begging bowls. As they walk the monks chant to let the villagers know they are on the way.

Villagers come out of their homes to make offerings to the monks to help support the monastery. When the villagers approach, the monks extend their begging bowls. Their big straw hats are over their eyes so the monks cannot see the person who is giving to them, and the person cannot see them. Giving and receiving are done anonymously. The monks do not want to shame anyone, or make them proud either, about their gift. Neither sees the other. As the monks bow and extend their begging bowl, one hand is giving, one is receiving, and in that moment, the two become one. This is a beautiful example of giving and receiving with a full and pure heart. We see the balance between giving and receiving, two parts of the same hand.

When one finds they cannot give or receive freely, it is time to look at what they are holding onto.

Practice: What do you give in relationships? What do you withhold?

Make a list of what you give in relationships and to whom.

And what do you refuse to give, and to whom?

So often our giving is conditional. We feel someone must deserve or earn our gift.

But the sun gives warmth to all, no matter who steps beneath it. It is extremely powerful to give unconditionally when the moment or need arises. And, of course, as we do so, we are also giving to ourselves. When we give in this manner, there is nothing more we need to receive.

Pillar of Love: True Giving and Receiving Are One.

True giving and receiving are one. When we give fully, without wanting anything in return, we become full. There is no giver or receiver there, only an open heart. Once we are able to offer what we have to others, we will see that we do not lose anything at all. The world is continually offering itself to us as well.

We breathe in and breathe out every day. We take in air and return air to the universe. Every step we take contains both giving and receiving. In many moments of our lives we experience letting go, giving up what we have naturally.

Giving is not different from receiving; they are interlinked. If we give fully and completely, when the next moment comes we will have room to receive what is next. Without breathing out, we cannot breathe in. Ultimately we will see that it is the very act of holding on that keeps all true nourishment away.

As we learn to engage in this kind of giving and receiving we begin to taste the fruit of real love. Real love makes no claims or demands. It gives the loved one freedom to grow. Love cannot be taken away, as it does not belong to anyone. It is always available and as plentiful as the air we breathe.

The Zen master showed us the more we give the more we will be able to receive the incredible moon that is constantly shining on us all.

Receiving

Receiving is an art as well. Rather than be able to receive graciously, some demand, manipulate, sulk or are unaware of what is being given to them. They take everything for granted and look the other way. But true receiving is an art. If we cannot receive from another, we block their ability to be open and give.

Turning Point: Open Your Hands

In order to be able to receive joyously, we must open our hands, acknowledge the gift and offer thanks. We receive so many things we pay no attention to. We receive our breath. Who gave it? Where would we be without it? Where does it come from? Where does it go? What must we do to deserve it? Nothing. This breath is purely given, and purely received.

Did you receive breakfast this morning? Lunch? Did someone call to say hello? Did you receive the rays of the sun that were shining, or the smile of a woman who passed you on the street? Were you there to receive it? Were you willing to do so? Did you take a moment to stop and offer thanks? What else did you give in return? To whom?

Many of us block the gifts sent to us, do not truly receive them or give thanks. We may feel what we receive is our due, or that it is not good enough. We deserve more and better. Rather than feel grateful, we may be fuming inside.

Turning Point: Seeing What You Have Received and Giving Thanks Heals Deeply

This is a vitally different orientation from what we are used to. Here we see that lack, limitation and stinginess are not our intrinsic condition. We are continually being given to, and the more we are willing to give others, the fuller we become.

Practicing Giving and Receiving in Our Relationships

Exercise: Ask for What You Want

So many relationships flounder due to not understanding the true nature of giving and receiving. Many feel they are not being given to sufficiently, though their partners may not even know what it is they are yearning for. Others may feel too much is being demanded of them. They feel drained and still cannot say no.

A wonderful way to deal with this is to ask directly for what you want. Ask without criticism or a hidden demand. By letting your partner know how to please you, you are giving them a gift. It's also important to let your partner know what it is you can and cannot give in return.

You Cannot Say Yes If You Cannot Say No

When you ask, be willing to accept yes or no. Saying no is not rejection. We cannot truly say yes if we cannot say no. It is not necessary to fulfill every request. At times, saying no is a way of giving to yourself.

Exercise: What Kind of Gift Do You Want from Me?

If there is doubt and confusion in a relationship, simply ask:

"What kind of gift do you want from me?
Will you let me give it to you?"

Make sure to let your partner know what he or she is giving you now. Acknowledge the gifts you receive, and offer thanks.

If more is being requested than you can provide, simply say so.

When giving and receiving are not clear and mutual there is a block to healthy flow. When we find that we cannot give or take from another, then it is time to see that something destructive may be going on.

Turning Point: Practice Giving Whatever Is Needed

It's fascinating to notice what we will give and what we won't. And to whom. Just notice it.

Then turn it around. Give unexpected gifts to people you don't usually give to.

Make sure you are giving freely, not expecting anything back in return.

Start little by little. This practice will free you immensely.

See what happens as this practice goes on. See if you are willing to receive the immense gifts the universe is constantly bestowing.

The Practice of Naikan

There is a wonderful practice called Naikan, developed in Japan, dedicated to the art of giving and receiving. Naikan turns around our usual way of thinking and being. The mind is wired to constantly focus upon all that we lack, how others have maligned us, how we've been wronged. Most of the time we feel we are giving so much and receiving so little, when often the opposite is true.

Naikan breaks our focus upon all that we lack, and puts our attention instead on what we are receiving and giving thanks to. Naikan also naturally repairs what has gone wrong in our lives.

A practice session of Naikan can last about thirty to forty minutes. (There are also Naikan retreats available, where it can be done all day long.)

In this practice there are three questions we ask ourselves. We dwell upon these questions each day and write all our answers down. Sometimes the answers will arise later on; whenever they do is perfect.

Question 1: What Did I Receive Today?

First we do Naikan with the day. Spend time with this question and be specific. Write down everything you've received today. Most of time we feel bereft and empty, as if we haven't received much.

We receive so many things we pay no attention to. We receive our breath. Who gave it? Where would we be without it? Where does it come from? Where does it go? What must we do to deserve it? Nothing. This breath is purely given, and purely received.

Did you receive breakfast this morning? Lunch? Did someone call to say hello? Did you receive the rays of the sun as it was shining, or the smile of a woman who passed you on the street? Were you there to receive it? Where you willing to do so? Write it all down.

Many of us block the gifts given to us, do not acknowledge them. We may feel they are our due, or that they are not good enough. We deserve more and better. Rather than feel grateful, we may be fuming inside.

Seeing what you have, receiving it, and giving thanks for it is one of the most healing practices of all. As we embark upon this practice and do it daily, we stop overlooking the endless gifts that we are receiving all the time.

Question 2: What Did I Give Today?

This question can be very surprising. Most of think we're giving all day long and receiving very little. But as we do the exercise, it can be a shock to see that we didn't give as much as we thought. Maybe we actually gave very little. Did we stop and greet the person we knew on the street, or even nod in passing? Did we give them a smile? A warm hello? Write it all down.

What else did we give? To whom? As we dwell upon this day by day, and also become aware of all that we are receiving, we soon become very eager to give more. We actually look forward for opportunities to do so.

Question 3: What Trouble or Pain Did I Cause Today?

Most of the time we focus upon the wrongs others have done us, how we have been misused or maligned. This question turns around the focus of the mind, as we become aware of how we may have inadvertently hurt another, or caused them trouble we were not conscious of. As we see this, our own anger, entitlement and self-righteousness dissolve. Instead, we become eager to correct our errors and amend our ways. The purpose of this exercise is not to create guilt, but to widen our focus, see our own actions clearly.

We make a third list of any trouble or pain we may have caused anybody. Some think this list will induce guilt. It may or it may not. But guilt is a waste of time and not the purpose of the exercise. Guilt makes us feel as though we've done something to correct a situation when we haven't. We've just punished ourselves.

A much better response is to notice that we have caused difficulty or pain, and then to simply correct it. Apologize, acknowledge it, offer something to heal the situation. And, also, when we are aware of the ways in which we cause trouble or pain we are much less likely to do it again.

Some ways in which we may have caused trouble can include simple acts like sending the waiter back over and over to change our dinner, not answering a call in a timely manner, simple acts we've done without realizing its effects upon others. And of course there are other acts that must be tended to, other realizations as well.

It's so freeing to realize that what we've done can be corrected quickly and easily. Even if someone has passed away, we can still make the correction. We can take what we've learned from the situation with the person and make an offering of what we've learned from it, to help others now. We can harvest our errors so they become fertilizer and help us make other lives better.

Naikan provides a vitally different orientation from what we're used to. Here we see that suffering is not our intrinsic nature. It arises from unawareness of what we are giving and receiving, how we are behaving, deep self-absorption. Instead we can turn our focus around, and open our world up completely.

We can also do Naikan on a person or relationship. Go over the relationship, three years at a time, at one sitting. Ask, what did I receive from that person, what did I give, and what trouble or pain did I cause?

Doing this practice daily has enormous effects. It is said it was founded by a physician in Japan who left his medical practice to go from home to home, helping others do Naikan. Many of his patients were healed.

"Give, give recklessly. We are only part of an endless process with nothing to gain or lose. Only to live it out."

Henry Miller

CHAPTER 10

Feeding the Hungry Ghost

*"Feeding Others
We Are Fed."*

Uchiyama

(Nourishing Ourselves and Others)

Feeding Others, We Are Fed

It's delicious to feel well-nourished in relationships. There's a yearning and hunger we bring to our partners for all kinds of food: warmth, kindness, appreciation, time spent together. However, many of us enter relationships starving, as a hungry ghost. No matter how much our partner gives us, it is never enough.

A hungry ghost is someone who has been invited to a banquet where there are all kinds of foods. But no matter how much they eat, they never feel full. They cannot swallow the food, taste or digest it. So they just keep eating more and more.

This is also true in relationships where we go from one person to the next hoping they will fill our empty hearts. We turn to our partners, much as we turned to our parents, hoping they'll provide nourishment.

However, when this nourishment is not forthcoming, some will do anything to get fed.

Pillar of Love: Another Person Can Never Fill You Up.

In order to understand the true workings of relationships, how to feel full, we must understand what truly nourishes and what leaves us even more hungry and empty than before. And we must deeply understand that another person can never fill us up. It is something within ourselves that is keeping us from tasting and digesting all that we are taking in.

Poison One: Greed

"Give Me More. The More the Better."

Many lives are based on unrecognized greed—*the more the better* is our mantra.

Somehow, what we have is never enough. We live our lives in order to consume, accumulate, store up treasures, possessions, titles, relationships, funds, and hoard them. We are taught to accumulate as much as we can, no matter what the cost, or at whose expense. Then we identify with our possessions and ultimately feel they are who we are. But is this so?

As we do this, we lose touch with our basic nature and true needs. The further out of touch we are, the hungrier and more desperate we become; as a hungry ghost now we are continually seeking more and more. In this frame of mind, whatever we receive only satisfies momentarily, then we are onto the next.

There are all kinds of different things a hungry ghost can get caught up in. It can be craving for love, money, prestige, sex, relationships. There are addictions of many kinds. As we demand, crave and cling to our experiences we make them the basis of our self-worth. That process itself is damaging.

Feeding the Hungry Ghost

On and on we go, trying to feed the hungry ghost within (or trying to feed someone else in a relationship who is a hungry ghost and cannot be satisfied). Many feel as though they've failed with a partner like that. But no matter how much we give, the hungry ghost can never be filled up. They just feel the gnawing hunger and want more and more.

In order to feel satisfied with our food, it's necessary to taste each bite, digest it thoroughly, receive the nourishment from it and discard the waste. This is not only true of a meal of food on the table, but the great meal of life itself, including our relationships.

Turning Point: Taste and Digest Both Your Food And Life Fully

Practice: View your life as a great meal you are being offered. Don't just gulp experiences down, wanting more and more to fill yourself up. Stop and taste whatever is happening. Give yourself time to digest it, appreciate it, receive the nourishment each experience offers. Give yourself a chance to absorb what's happened. Don't keep searching for what's next.

The Great Value of Empty Space

Soen Roshi, a great master, said, "Usually when we want to see the beauty of a room, we decorate it, fill it up, add all kinds of furnishings and decorations. Then we look at what's in the room, to appreciate the beauty. We do the same thing in our lives. So many of us are afraid of emptiness, both without and within."

However, in Zen practice, the opposite happens. We remove things from the room, one by one, eliminate clutter. Then we can see the true beauty of the original, empty space. This open, empty space contains everything, and the natural beauty of the room is beyond compare.

It is of the upmost importance to make room for the openness, emptiness, and silence in our lives as well. Once we do, we will have the space to taste, digest what we have been given. And when we are truly able to taste our food and life, we become deeply satisfied with even just one sip of tea. The less we cling to, the less clutter is around us, the more we can appreciate what is right here now.

It was early morning, the third day of a meditation retreat, and the usual breakfast of oatmeal was about to be served. We sat in meditation and extended our small bowls to be filled. As every other day, the server placed a few spoonfuls of oatmeal in my bowl. When the bell sounded, it was time for us all to eat together. I lifted my bowl and placed a small amount of plain oatmeal in my mouth.

But today was different! As I took a mouthful, I was stunned. Suddenly, for the first time in my life, I truly tasted the oatmeal. How incredibly delicious it was. Filled with wonder, I sobbed. Although I'd eaten oatmeal for years, I'd never tasted it before. How much else of life had I just gulped down? My tears fell and fell.

Practice: Give Things Away

Make space in your home, your life, your heart. Then you can better taste and feel all you are being given. Give things away. Do not accumulate. Do the opposite, remove all kinds of clutter and let go of whatever is unnecessary now. Soon you will deeply value the empty space; you won't be able to do without it.

And, as Soen Roshi suggested, to discover the beauty of your home and life, start emptying it out. Clean your inner and outer home thoroughly, give things away. The more empty space in your life, the freer you will be to move around and see new possibilities.

Just do it slowly, one thing at a time. Doing everything at once with great urgency, feeling there's no time to accomplish anything, can simply be another form of greed. Much better to relish each step you take.

Finally, you will have enough room to see what is in front of you and uncover your original nature. This is an ongoing process, to let go of all that is unimportant, the clutter, painful memories, anger, confusion, accumulations that block your natural beauty and spaciousness.

Feeding the Hungry Heart

Being Fed and Being Loved

Naturally, the hungry ghost is not just hungry for food, but for love. From the moment we are born, we connect being fed with being loved. When we cry, mother comes and feeds us and we feel safe and cared for. If the food we need is withheld for too long, we scream in pain. This pattern can continue throughout an entire life.

In some relationships one person consistently plays the role of the feeder and other the role of the one being fed. Some withhold the nourishment needed until their partners do what they want. Others feed their partners on demand. Sex is often used in this fashion, providing a sense of being loved, wanted, cared for and nourished. When it is withheld or rationed out, the hungry partner feels devastated.

Most are not aware of the many kinds of nourishment the universe abundantly provides. As in childhood, they become fixated on one person, whom they see as their sole source of well-being. This is the idea of the infant; take care of me and all will be well.

What Kind of Food Are We Consuming?

It is also necessary to stop a moment and recognize exactly what kind of food we are consuming. Is it healthy, can our system digest it? Although fast food may taste good and initially fill us up, it can have bad side effects. Although what we get from our partner is initially hot and spicy it can cause heartburn later on. We can eat all day and never receive the nourishment needed.

Many individuals feel inadequate and like failures in relationships because they feel they haven't given enough or made their partner happy. But it is impossible to make another happy, or to fulfill their needs. We must be aware of all kinds of nourishment, emotional, mental and spiritual, that is given and received, and what it really means to take care of another.

Zen Cooking: Feeding Others We Are Fed

In order to receive the nourishment we desire in relationships, it's good to learn how to become the cook, how to nourish, provide for and feed others.

In the zendo the cook is called the tenzo. During retreats the tenzo may have to feed fifty people or more, three times a day. The meals must be cooked with great mindfulness and care, with not a drop of food wasted. The meals also must be served at exactly the right moment, when the bell rings out. This cooking itself becomes a deep training in awareness and offering, not only food, but one's entire self. When one is in this state of being, it is impossible to be hungry or discontent.

Feeding Others: What Can Be Offered

Being the cook means learning how to appreciate the needs of others and being willing to completely fill them, on time. Rather than compulsively focusing upon on our own hunger, we attend to the needs of others. As we do this, a strange thing happens: feeding others, we are fed ourselves.

We are then able to relish life and people, as they are given. Our relationships turn around one hundred and eighty degrees. It no longer becomes a question of what the other is or isn't giving. It's a question of what can be offered to him or to her.

Turning Point: Develop Parental Mind

Parental Mind

Parental mind, a phrase coined by Uchiyama Roshi, is the state of mind that wants to care for and nourish others. It is the mind of the mother with a newborn child with unconditional regard for the child. It is not a mind which keeps accounts or continually needs to be filled up and attended to.

As we live from parental mind there is a never-ending source of nourishment that exists within. No matter who does or does not give to us, we need never feel empty or deprived again.

Developing Parental Mind

In order to develop parental mind, we don't choose one person and reject another. The homeless man on the street is just as precious as our own child. Though this attitude may seem impossible to adopt in the beginning, with time, patience, and steady practice, this kind of mind naturally grows. When you are rejecting someone, stop and notice what's happening. You are depriving yourself of an opportunity to see something wonderful, and to learn and grow.

Naturally, relationships fluctuate. Sometimes we love someone very much, and then they behave in ways we don't like and our feelings change. Before long they may even seem like an enemy. Our task, however, is to understand and develop the true nature of friendship, or kindness, unconditional regard.

Pillar of Love: The More We Attend to the Needs Of Others, the More Complete and Full We Feel.

Practice: Being Nourished in Relationships

What kind of food are you taking in your relationship?

Is it nourishing for you?

Can you digest it?

What do you provide for others?

Take a look and see.

Practice: How May I Serve You?

This is a wonderful practice in and of itself, recommended by Zen Master Charlotte Joko Beck. Simple and powerful, it cuts through relationship tangles and focuses on what we're here for.

In the midst of anger, upset, even accusations, simply ask (either in your mind or out loud), *"How May I Serve You?"*

How can you be a force for healing, light and clarity in the relationship? It will be different for each person and each situation. Now we are developing true generosity of heart.

Practice: Real Generosity

Who is the most generous person you know?

Why? What is it about them?

When are you most generous? What allows you to be this way?

"Real generosity is the state of mind where one lets the other just be."

Trungpa

Apples or Pears?

Clea spent all her time wanting to change Arnold. "There's so much that's wonderful about him," she said, "but what I'm hungering for I don't get. I need more excitement."

Rather than go to another relationship, where she could get the "excitement" she thought she wanted, she stayed with Arnold, feeling dissatisfied.

It was as though Arnold were an apple tree who was giving her fabulous apples, while she was all the time longing for pears. Rather than walk down the street to the pear tree and take one, she railed against this fine apple tree, which could not produce a pear, no matter how hard it tried.

Addicted to Not Getting What We Want

Some of us are simply addicted to *not* getting what we want and being dissatisfied. We prefer to rail against the apple tree instead of thanking it for its beautiful apples, and choosing to go and find a pear tree if we need pears. We'll go to one apple tree after another with the same complaint, begging it to produce pears, making it feel inadequate because it can't.

Pillar of Love: You Will Never Turn an Apple Tree into a Pear Tree. Give Up Trying.

Turning Point: Allow a Person To Be Who They Are

Practice: Recognize Each One's Essential Worth

Thank a person for what they do give you. Recognize and value their essential worth.

If we spend all our time wanting to change the person, rejecting their essential qualities, not wanting or valuing what they give, this is a surefire recipe for misery, for everyone concerned.

Are we able to absorb what is wonderful in the relationship and discard the rest? Can we take in the beauty and value offered, and bypass that which is not valuable? Some can, others not.

Honor and be grateful for that which you receive. Why become bitter spending all your time focusing upon that which the person is not able to provide?

If your partner is giving you wonderful apples and you are desperately craving a pear, don't attack the apples. You are with an apple tree and it's doing its best. Thank the apple tree for its beautiful apples. If you must have a pear, find a pear tree, walk down the street. It's right there.

Turning Point: Give Up Searching for Apples on a Pear Tree

Practice: Recognize What You Are Receiving and Give Thanks

Notice what some of the apple trees you keep returning to when you're hungry for pears. What is the outcome?

Where are the pear trees in your life? What is it that you hunger for? What nourishes you most? Can you allow yourself to have it? And give thanks?

> *"The real battle is inner, and is nothing but a battle*
> *Between the real and ideal man."*

CHAPTER 11

Giving Thanks

"In the time to come all prayers will cease,
but the prayer of thanksgiving will not cease."

The Banquet of Life

Some would say that this world is like a banquet in which we are guests. However, instead of thoroughly enjoying the feast, we become upset that the meal will not last forever. We criticize everything, the cook, the food, the other guests. We want one dish and not another. Or, we gorge ourselves with the wrong meal for us and then wonder why we become ill.

Many people spend their entire time at the feast looking for unpleasant things about the others. They have no idea at all who their host is, or why they have been invited in the first place. Most of the time they never think of offering thanks.

Some do not care at all about what they are doing at this enormous feast. When the food runs out, they simply feel terrified. Others don't care so much about the food, they just want to push the other guests around. They are under the illusion that this is their party and do not yet realize that all have been invited here to partake equally in the feast.

Some refuse the meal entirely and go to the corner to pout, waiting for the party to end.

Pillar of Love: Your Life Is a Banquet; Enjoy the Feast.

Developing a Grateful Mind

It may take a while to realize that one reason we have been invited to this party is to develop a grateful mind. We must learn to partake of the offering and offer thanks. And, after we eat our fill, it is natural to ask what we can offer in return.

What Can I Offer in Return?

It is also important to realize that at this banquet each person is precious and has been invited for a reason. There is something unique each guest has to contribute, including ourselves. It is also important to remember that one day we will all be departing. This banquet does not last forever. Each moment is precious.

In Zen practice, over and over again we put our hands together and make a little bow. This is a bow of both acknowledgment and thanks. We take time to notice and fully appreciate what is before us. Then, with our entire mind and body, we stop to give thanks.

Giving thanks is crucial; just taking and taking is not enough. As we develop a mind that is aware of the gifts it is receiving, and gives thanks, the grateful mind develops.

The Best Medicine There Is

There is one surefire medicine which cures all difficulty and opens the way for the greater good. It allows you to sleep well at night, wake up refreshed and filled with enthusiasm. Obstacles evaporate and wonderful encounters appear. This medicine is abundantly available, has no side effects, and can be taken in large or small doses regularly. You need no one to prescribe it and the more you take, the sweeter it is.

A grateful mind is the best medicine available. Not only does it have only beneficial side effects, but it benefits everyone with whom it comes in touch. The grateful mind has the ability to give and receive truly and expresses itself naturally in the practice of thankfulness.

Pillar of Love: You Cannot Be Grateful and Depressed at the Same Time.

If you are having difficulty in your relationships, be aware that depression and gratitude cannot co-exist. If you are continually aware of the good you are receiving, complaints, resentment and demands become a thing of the past. When this is not happening, the question must be, what am I focusing on right now? Where is my attention?

Turning Point: Your Focus Can Build or Destroy Your Life

As You Take Charge of Your Focus, You Take Charge of Your Life

As you take charge of your focus you take charge of your life. What you focus upon will determine your feelings, thoughts and deeds. Your focus builds or destroys your relationships and your life.

Are you focusing upon all your problems, or are you aware of the endless gifts you receive daily? By taking your attention off the negative aspects of your relationships, you take energy and power away from these complaints and become open to see the good that is available. You will also see what it is you are truly giving and receiving right now.

The Incredible Taste of Kindness

The Tree Roshi

Many years ago a great teacher, known as the Tree Roshi, lived in a tree, secluded and meditating for many years. After his great awakening, not only birds flocked around him, but people from all over were drawn to him. Great groups of people gathered and begged him to come down out of the tree house and share his wisdom with them. Finally, he had no choice.

The Tree Roshi climbed back down to earth, sat with others and listened to their needs.

"Please tell us what you have learned," they begged of him.

"Whatever is harmful to you, do not do to another," he replied simply. "Whatever would bring you benefit, do to others as well."

"Is that it?" The people were disappointed. "Even an eight-year-old child knows that," they complained.

"Yes," answered the Tree Roshi. "Even an eight-year-old child knows it, but even an eighty-year-old man cannot do it."

The fruit of all true practice is kindness, both to others and to ourselves. It is easy to speak and read about kindness; it is another to make it into your flesh and bones. What is kindness, really? How does it appear and function in this world, and why is it so hard for an eighty-year-old man who has been practicing his whole life to obey the simple teaching?

Kindness does not arise from the logical mind. It arises from another part of ourselves and can often become confused with Counterfeit Compassion.

Counterfeit Compassion

In Zen we find a notion of idiot compassion, which describes someone who thinks that by adopting an external show of kindness, they are truly benefiting someone. They may give a crying child candy to wipe his tears away, perhaps not realizing that the child is diabetic and that the candy may do great harm. Or a person may extend a helping hand to another, which, in fact, may weaken or enslave them. At times an individual may need to be rebuffed and pushed away, so that they might learn how to stand tall on their own. Rote kindness is not helpful. We all need different forms of kindness at different periods of time in our lives.

In all walks of life we find the obvious appearances of kindness; encouraging words, smiles, displays of emotion and concern. However, the external appearance of kindness is one thing. True acts of kindness are something else.

True compassion arises naturally as we let go of self-centered absorption and become aware of and mindful of others and what is truly here now. When we give what is truly needed, and do not dwell upon our own particular desires, right action and continual thanks arise on their own.

Turning Point: Give Thanks Constantly

When a great rabbi was asked who a true Jew was, he replied: **"He Or She Who Gives Thanks Constantly."**

When we are aware of the great gifts we receive all the time, stop, appreciate them, and offer thanks, it is truly impossible to be sad and depressed. What a simple and powerful antidote to depression. Why aren't we all doing it?

Practice: Many Ways of Giving Thanks

There are many ways of giving thanks, some that are widespread and some that can be unique to you. Let's take a look at the ways you give thanks, and how you feel as you do so.

Make a list of the ways in which you give thanks.

Make a list of the people you give thanks to.

Take note of the ways in which others thank you. Are you aware of it when they are doing so?

Take note of the ways you feel when you are not noticed or thanked for your offering.

This is very important. It is an opportunity to remember that the highest way of true giving is to forget about receiving anything in return from the one you have given to.

Your offering is your way of giving thanks. Responses come and will come in all different kinds of ways.

Turning Point: The Ultimate Thank You

Now we are about to approach a most intense and powerful way of offering honor, respect and thanks to others. It is also a wonderful way to eliminate your own arrogance and pride. This is a practice that can be done every day, to all we encounter. When done with a full heart it instantly turns the moment around.

Practice: Before You Interact, Bow to the Person (In Your Mind)

Bowing represents a relinquishing of ego and arrogance and the willingness to honor others. It is a surrender of the personal self, an offering of deep respect for all life. Bowing is full acknowledgment of the other, and of the value and worth of the universe we live together in. It is a way of saying I honor you, value you, thank you. I do not put myself on top of you, or as superior in any way. We are always together in this wild dance of life. Bowing recognizes that our self-centered desires, delusions, pride and arrogance have no reality; they only make our lives bitter.

We can bow to a person, a room, an animal, a bird, a tree outside the window. When we bow we stop and acknowledge the value and beauty of what is before us. It is recognition that we are not the center of the entire world, but are willing to respect, honor and serve it.

*"Bowing is a very serious practice. You should be
prepared to bow, even in your last moment. Even
though it is impossible to get rid of our self-centered
desires, we have to do it. Our true nature wants us to."*

Suzuki Roshi

By bowing we are giving ourselves up, letting go of separation. When you bow to another, you become one with them. When you are one with everything that exists, you are one with the divine and find the true meaning of being.

"Sometimes a man bows to a woman, sometimes a woman bows to a man. Sometimes the disciple bows to the master; sometimes the master bows to the disciple. Sometimes the master and disciple bow together. Sometimes we may bow to cats and dogs.

"Bowing helps eliminate our self-centered ideas. This is not so easy. It is difficult to get rid of these ideas, and bowing is a very valuable practice. The result is not the point; it is the effort to improve ourselves that is valuable."

Suzuki Roshi

Practice: Bowing to Everyone
Today, bow in your mind (or physically if you care to) to every person you have an interaction with. Before you start interacting with the person, take a moment and bow in your mind. See how this changes the quality of the interaction. See how it affects the quality of your day.

Bow to Those You Have Difficulty With

Make a point of bowing (in your mind or physically) to three people you are having difficulty with. Keep doing it until the difficulty is gone.

Bow Before Fighting

Just as a fight is about to begin between you and someone else, stop a moment and bow, (either physically or in your mind). Then see how you feel. Bow to your desk before you sit down to work at it, bow to your food, to your friends, your car. Bow to the morning, stop and bow to a sunset.

This simple exercise will open your heart. Years ago a group of police officers who worked in Times Square were taking a class on self-change. This exercise was given to them as homework. One of the students in the class resonated with the exercise strongly.

He had a late shift on that weekend. Before he knew it there was a scuffle and he had to rush over to arrest someone. Just before he arrested the individual, the officer remembered his homework and was struck with the idea of bowing to him.

He bowed to the man in his mind deeply before he reached out to arrest him. The man swiftly looked up and suddenly they looked into one another's eyes. The police officer said he was thunderstruck.

He saw a person, not a criminal, in front of him, and was filled with deep caring for him. The person began crying and the officer reached out in a completely different way. The interaction between them changed the police officer's life.

When we truly see what is before us, it is impossible to remain as we've always been.

"Let us eliminate the doctor as well as the patient
By accepting the disease itself."

Henry Miller

CHAPTER 12

Extending a Helping Hand

"We get sick because we act in sickening ways."

Joruard

Another aspect of the practice of giving and receiving is extending a helping hand. As with all the other aspects of relationships, true helping may look a bit different than we imagine. There are ways to give that truly uplift another and there are other ways that create weakness, dependency and shame. Once again, it's vital to explore the practice of true helping, to look more deeply at what it is that heals, balances and uplifts us all.

Helpers want to help. They feel it is their job to make a person better and that the more they intervene, the more they are helping. Their motives are often excellent. Their goal is to offer relief, respite, comfort. Although the goal is valuable, very few first stop and ask the basic question:

What is the true cause of the suffering?
What is true kindness?
What does this person really need from me?

Most helpers seek to remove symptoms, stop the pain. They attempt to put things back together again the way they were. This, of course, is based upon the assumption that things were fine as they were, or that pain is bad or is a signal that something has gone awry in the person's body or mind. But this is not necessarily true. Pain can be a great teacher, a wakeup call, a way to connect with parts of ourselves that we have long overlooked or disowned.

Pain can be a gift from our larger selves, our inner wisdom, warning us that we are out of balance in ways we never imagined, and that there is a larger direction for our lives, one we are presently out of touch with.

Pain Is Simply Pain: Suffering Is Optional

Pillar of Love: There Is a Difference Between Pain and Suffering.

To truly help, it is important to understand that there is a difference between pain and suffering. Pain is simply pain. Suffering is what we add to it. Pain cannot be avoided in life. To try to avoid it is part of the problem The more we are able to experience and accept our pain, the sooner it subsides. We do not need to explain pain away. We cannot figure it out. We can, however, receive it.

In the simple receiving, pain transforms into something quite different. Not only does the pain transform, but more importantly, so do we.

Do Not Run Away from Painful Moments

If we spend our lives running away from painful moments, we shut out a great deal of what life brings us, both the painful and joyful. When we are willing to accept our experience, just as it is, a strange thing happens: our experience changes into something else. When we avoid pain, struggle not to feel it, pain turns into suffering. There is an enormous difference between pain and suffering. Pain often cannot be avoided. Suffering can. As we learn the difference between them, many fears subside.

Never Impose Your Idea of What Helping Is Upon Another

It is dangerous to think that "I am the helper," that you know better what is needed than the person who needs assistance. It is not up to you to impose your notion of what help is upon another.

There is a wonderful story about Martin Buber, who was a great rabbi and theologian. Many came to him with questions, problems, seeking guidance and advice of all kinds. And he studied hard to find good answers.

Then one day, a young man came to see him with his questions as well. The young man asked his questions, and as every other day, Martin Buber listened to him and offered his knowledge. Then a few hours after the meeting, the young man went home and hung himself.

When Martin Buber discovered this he was devastated, completely shocked. He closed his books, left his office, and spent days and days dwelling upon the following question.

> **"What does a person truly need when they are feeling desperation and come to another for help?"**

This was not a question he could find an answer to in a book. It became a koan for him and he thought of nothing else. Finally, after a long period of time, sudden clarity came.

What a person needs is a Presence, through which they know that nevertheless, there is meaning.

After realizing this so deeply, Martin Buber put away all his books and ready-made answers and spent the rest of his life becoming completely Present to each person and situation as it came to him. This became his lifelong practice. To be there for them entirely, not thinking of answers, not judging who they were. He realized that he didn't know who they were, but also that his true, full and unwavering Presence could become a bridge to meaning, comfort and connection. His Presence could provide the strength needed so the person would feel heard, known and not alone.

"Who You Are Speaks So Loud I Can't Hear What You Say"

On the deepest level, it's not what you *say*, it's who you *are* that creates an environment where real help takes place. Preaching at others means little. People hear the message of your being, who you are, what your life is, as soon as they are with you. They know if they can trust you, if your words and deeds are aligned. They also know if you are helping in order to feel virtuous or superior to them, or to exert control. That attitude will never work.

Pillar of Love: Get Rid of the Idea That You Can Heal Anyone.

No one can ever heal another. No one can even imagine what healing truly means for another person at a point in their lives. You do not have their answers. Only the person themselves know.

There is *One Within Each of Us That Knows The Way*. We do great damage to others and to ourselves by disrespecting this reality. We offer great support and courage when we help the other make the acquaintance of *The Wisdom and Strength Within*.

A *true helper* creates a healing environment, where there is trust, strength and calm. They are fully aware that they are not better, wiser or stronger than the one they are helping. They never make the person feel weak or inadequate in any way. By creating the illusion of dependency and weakness, the helper is causing harm.

"I am sick because all beings are sick."

Vimilarkirti

We all suffer and heal together

Fundamentally, we are all connected. We all suffer and heal together as well. The true basis for helping arises when we are able to help the person fully welcome and trust and listen to their strength and wisdom within.

Pillar of Love: The Job of a Helper Is to Accompany the Person on Their Journey.

Turning Point: Do Not Interfere

The job of a helper is to accompany the person on the journey they are on, to lend support and courage, not to judge, correct, or interfere with what's going on for them. When we interfere, impose upon, or categorize another, we are diminishing their ability to discover their own needs and strength. And we are robbing them of trust in themselves.

A group of Zen students were practicing zazen together during a sesshin, a seven-day retreat. At times much pain rose up and could be intense. All of a sudden one student could no longer maintain the silence and stillness and burst into loud tears.

The Zen master immediately called out, "Do not interfere with his precious suffering." By sitting together in the silence, unmoving, the students were extending huge support. In fact, it was what permitted this student to go through the pain. He was not alone with his experience; they were all there beside him, respecting him and allowing his journey to take its course.

Practice: Notice how much you want to change or interfere with the distress of others. Give it up.

You Do Not Have Anyone Else's Answer

In order to find answers and easily solve conflict, what is needed up front is an atmosphere which facilitates listening, safety and trust. Part of creating that atmosphere is being fully aware that you are not better or wiser than the person you are listening do. You do not know more than them or have their answer. What they need is not your answer, but a space of listening and respect in which they can experience their own truth.

The Gift of Self-Trust

It is crucial to never make another feel inadequate in any way. Do not interfere, comment or offer ready-made solutions. You are then imposing yourself upon the speaker, interrupting their journey and possibly even robbing them of faith and trust in themselves. This becomes an impediment. It is your job to simply accompany the speaker on their journey, like a wayfarer.

Instead of jumping in and trying to correct a situation, stop. Be silent and still and fully be with the other, and be with yourself. If they wish to speak to you, fully listen, without offering suggestions. Don't listen to your own inner chatter; listen to them.

By truly listening, you are giving comfort, strength and support. You are also creating a non-judgmental, open environment where the person becomes able to hear themselves as well.

Turning Point: Develop Trust in Yourself

Trust in oneself is one of the most powerful medicines available. Yet all of society conspires to take that away. Why is it so dangerous? How can we reclaim it for ourselves and others? These are the questions that helpers must dwell upon.

Most advocate trusting external authorities and formulations of all kinds. We are expected to follow accepted procedures, do what is expected, when each of us has the key to what it is we are truly needing right now.

Lack of trust in ourselves is the disease we are suffering from.

Practice: Notice each time trust in yourself wavers, and see what has caused it to happen. What are you putting your trust in? Something someone said, something you've heard or read? Notice this and listen for your own inner knowingness.

Turning Point: Know the Difference Between Medicine and Poison

As we develop trust in ourselves we become able to know the difference between medicine and poison. Some give poison thinking they are giving medicine. It can be tricky, too, as medicine turns to poison and poison to medicine, all the time. What was wonderful for you yesterday may be awful today. Different times and conditions require different responses. It is crucial to be aware in the moment now. Most of us have it mixed up.

Practice: Are You Helping or Harming?

Be willing to see if what you are offering another truly helps or harms. Discover what it is that the person truly needs. Vigilance is needed. What has been good for someone may no longer be useful. What has been painful may suddenly cause someone to grow. It is necessary to be awake to what is happening in the other person, what is truly needed and wanted right now.

Take some time to dwell upon what is poison and what is medicine, what is beneficial and what can cause yourself or the other harm.

When Medicine Turns into Poison

However, most of us live in the world not knowing what is medicine and what is poison. We don't know what we really need, what will make us strong, healthy, clear and compassionate or what will cause a lot of anguish. So we live in a great deal of confusion. We think if something tastes good, it is going to be good for us. If we like a person, if they're sweet, kind, charming, it's medicine. We want to run to that kind of person for food or experience. We go to whatever tastes sweet and delicious, and then things suddenly change and we become dismayed.

Pillar of Love: What Is Sweet Is Not Necessarily Beneficial; What Is Bitter Is Not Necessarily Bad.

Turning Point: Do Not Avoid Bitterness

When a person is in a relationship that seems so sweet and lovely, where everything they want is being supplied, the person may not understand why they are feeling worse, becoming weaker, more dependent, or increasingly frightened that the partner will go away. If the situation is weakening you, it's poison.

On the other side, we can become involved with people and situations that are terrifically bitter, that we don't like. These are painful and we want to run away. And yet there may be wonderful strength waiting here for us, important lessons we need to learn.

A True Companion

A Zen master had a nephew who was having a difficult time. His brother asked him to come and spend a week with the family and help the son. The Zen master agreed, and the nephew was nervous about how he would now be scolded. Once the Zen master arrived though, he said nothing at all about his nephew's difficulties. Instead, he enjoyed being in his nephew's company and accompanied him wherever he went. When the nephew went to a bar at night, the Zen master went along. When the nephew went to rowdy parties, the uncle accompanied him there as well. All the time the nephew waited to be reprimanded, scolded and set right.

The Zen master never said a word though. He simply accompanied his nephew and experienced outing after outing with him. This went on for a week. The nephew kept waiting for the sword to fall, but it never happened. Finally, it was time for the Zen master to go home. The nephew came to say good-bye and saw his uncle in his room, bending down to tie his shoes. As the Zen master looked up and saw his nephew, a tear rolled down his cheek. That's all.

Seeing that tear, the nephew was stunned. He couldn't move or speak. The simple, natural, spontaneous, heartfelt response of his uncle totally turned his life around. It is said that the nephew couldn't go back to his old way of life again, no matter how hard he tried.

Turning Point: Just Accompany The Other; No Comments Needed

The job of a helper is to accompany the person on the journey they are on, to lend support and courage, not to judge, correct, or interfere. When we judge, label or categorize another we are diminishing their natural ability to discover their own truth and to heal. And we are robbing them of trust in themselves.

A helper accompanies the person on their journey, wherever that person wants to go. They accompany them without preconceived ideas about how the person should be or their destination.

Practice: Train in Your Own Authenticity

The job of a helper is to work on themselves until this is their true state of being and they do not have to shut any person down. What the helper is really doing now is training in their own authenticity. The reward is to take many journeys with others, journeys they might never have embarked upon themselves. And to thank the person for having offered that opportunity. Helping others is a gift you are being given. Handle it with care.

Practice: Stop the Moment You See Something Wrong, Sick or Bad about Someone. Realize that is *your* perception, not necessarily them. Change your perception. Do Not Interfere.

"There is no progress
Other than what is,
If we could let it be."

CHAPTER 13

Training in Your Own Authenticity

"He affected everything
Not by dominating the scene,
But just by being true."

Pillar of Love: You Have Nothing to Give But Who You Are.

Those who wish to help must train in their own authenticity. The truth of who you are cannot be hidden. When we live from our truth, the split between what we know and who we are vanishes. We do not speak and think one way and act another. We manifest what is true.

"Who You Are Speaks So Loud I Can't Hear What You Say."

The Split Self

The greatest psychological pain we all suffer is the pain of being split, false, hidden, conflicted. This comes from knowing one thing and being, or living, another. Knowledge that has not been digested, absorbed into our very bones, becomes poison that we carry like an illness. That is why the emphasis in helping is not upon Knowing, but Being. It is not what you know, but who you are, that speaks volumes.

"Schizophrenia is not a break with reality. It is a break with sincerity."

Many live enclosed in layers of masks and games and then don't understand why they feel so lonely. But how can we be anything but lonely and cut off if we live behind a false persona, always trying to be something we're not? How can we do anything but feel suffocated, and suffocate others, by demanding they live that way as well?

Turning Point: Take Off Your Mask

As soon as our mask comes off, the light shines through. Life is fresh, constantly renewed, and we are too. These masks may not be so not easy to take off though. Although they constrict us at every turn, we'll fight to the death to keep them on. For some, the mask has become their identity. They think the mask they wear is their beauty and security. Without the mask they feel naked and bare. Some become so accustomed to wearing these masks that they confuse them with their very own skin, and with who they truly are.

We cling to masks and roles the way a drowning man clings to a lifeboat. If someone questions or insults our mask, we feel as though we are dying inside. Some would kill to uphold their public image. Some kill themselves when this image is gone.

Practice: Taking Off Masks

We create a mask to meet the masks of others. Then we wonder why we cannot love, and why we feel so alone.

Everything The Mask Says and Does Is For the Purpose of Hiding. True Communication Is For The Purpose of Love.

An Image Is a False Front, Concerned Only with the Reaction of Others.

An image is a false front, a false appearance. It is concerned only with the reaction of others to it. It wants to be seen and admired. It may want to fool others. This has nothing to do with real love. Can one mask love another? Does a mask know how to communicate? How Much of Your Mask Are You Willing to Relinquish? How Much Fresh Air Will You Let into Your Life?

Now let us look at our masks more closely. It is very interesting to notice which masks we have chosen to wear, which images we are trying to create.

Practice: What Kind of Masks Are You Hiding Behind?

False Faces

What Masks Have You Chosen to Wear? How Do You Want People to See You?

Most people see me as___.

I want others to see me as___.

Underneath my mask I am___.

Look at your responses carefully. What is your mask really doing for you?

Taking Off Our Masks

To love and be loved fully, we must let go of our masks. Masks keep us hidden and separate. Love shows that we are all one. Many find that the very act of taking off their masks is freeing, often fills them with love and joy.

What Mask Are You Wearing Today?

Look at Yourself in the Mirror Each Morning.

Notice Which Mask You Are Wearing Today.

Then, Look at the Person Underneath.

See Her/His Real Beauty.

Now, Imagine the Mask Slowly Dropping Away.

With a little practice, this will become easier and easier. It will be fun. And, to your surprise and delight, other stress dissolves quickly along with the false front you have been wearing. (It takes so much energy to keep a mask on.)

Once the masks and roles dissolve many become braver, freer, and more creative. Surprising solutions and insights appear. With a little persistence and patience it will only be a matter of a little while before your true person starts emerging into the light.

This is the person who knows how to love, how to discover the "right relationship."

This is the person who makes friends easily. Isn't it time you let him/her free?

Stop Living in a Make-Believe World

Along with wearing masks, there are many ways of living a false life. Throughout most of our lives we play a variation of the game of "Let's Pretend." Let's pretend that you didn't say that and I didn't hear. Let's pretend it all doesn't matter. I help you keep your pretenses up and you help me keep up mine. In one way this makes us feel safe and secure. In another, it robs our true life from us. We live in a make-believe world and become cardboard people. If someone knocks on our door to visit, most of the time there's no one home.

Pillar of Love: When We Need Help We Must Find Someone Home.

If Someone Knocks at Your Door, Are You There? Is Someone Home?

When we live presenting false fronts to others, we lose touch with who we truly are. When we retreat into roles and games the words we say will be empty. People will listen and not believe. Their sense of trust is impaired. When we are able to put our games, masks and roles aside, then true presence and love can arise.

Who Are We When Our Pretenses Are Gone?

Everyone fears being exposed. Some would rather die than have their masks and roles drop away. Even many of those who are quite ill are still primarily concerned about how they look to others and the impression they will make.

But as we grow older in life, the changes we encounter wipe out the images we hold of ourselves, and eventually take our masks, roles and games away. Who are we then when our pretenses are gone? Why is the *True Person* so hard to find and to live from day by day?

Turning Point: Meet the True Person of No Rank

To find the True Person of No Rank is a Zen koan. It means to find the real person within who is not defined by labels or titles of any kind. Not defined by their history or future plans.

Practice: Don't Be Someone, Just Be

At this moment, let all of it go. Don't be someone, just be. Be there for yourself and others. Stop playing familiar roles or trying to make an impression. You'll be amazed at how relaxed you'll feel, what a burden will be lifted from your shoulders. And how good others will feel around you as well.

> *"Give up, sirs, your proud airs and mannerisms,*
> *They won't do you any good,*
> *You do not need them,*
> *That's all I have to tell you."*
>
> *Lao Tsu*

The Roles We Play

In order to discover the true man of no rank, we must also look closely at the roles we play, the identities we cherish. These roles are often exactly what keep us so disconnected.

We wear many hats. In each hat we look and feel slightly different. These hats are comfortable. They ward off the wind, snow and rain. But sometimes one hat gets stuck on your head. You don't remember that you have just put it on for the afternoon, and that your face is hidden underneath.

Roles can be hypnotic. We can fall in love with a role or fantasy and begin to believe it is who we truly are. Or, more commonly, we can fall in love with someone who is playing a role. (Here we are not falling in love with the person, but with the image or fantasy he/she is creating for us.) It can come as quite a shock to us when the person drops his role and we are face to face with someone quite different.

The biggest danger of being lost in role-playing is that these roles may begin to play us, rather than vice versa. The role takes over and we can lose touch with the reality of what is going on at a particular moment. We may not be able to see the wide range of possibilities available, if we were able to respond truly.

An incredible amount of misunderstanding and lack of communication comes about through being glued to a particular role. Unglue yourself a little. See if you can begin to separate yourself from the static role definition you have been living with.

> *"A true man belongs to no time or place, but is the center of things. Where he is, there is nature."*
>
> *Emerson*

The Power of Authenticity

For many of us the idea of being true has become confused with the idea of being selfish, not caring about the feelings of others. Oddly enough, just the opposite is so. When we are able to respond truly, enormous caring begins to arise.

Also, our authenticity will strike a deep chord with our friend. This chord reverberates in many ways and much of the estrangement we feel in relationships disappears all by itself.

On the other hand, when we act from our roles, we are implicitly demanding a set response from the other as well. This kind of relating can be very deadening. Then we wonder why we feel so relieved when the other person goes away.

Practice: Letting Go of Roles

What roles do you love to play? Take a look at the roles you play regularly. Write them down.

Which do you enjoy the most?

Which roles are you afraid to play?

Pick a role you like the best. Play it with a partner for a few minutes. Now, reverse roles. Have your partner play your usual part. How does it feel to be on the other end?

By letting go of your role and just being present you open the way for the other to do so as well. You also open the way for a miracle, for a *Real Meeting* to take place. What happens to loneliness then?

Exercise: Drop All Labels

Just stop labeling others, defining them this way or that. Life is much larger than all the labels you have for it, which puts everything into a tidy, manageable box. What we don't see is that when we are busy labeling others, we are constricting and labeling ourselves as well.

As you do this, what happens to your identity? The opposite of what you'd expect. You're not more vulnerable, you're stronger. You're no longer identified in a limited way. Instead, if you look carefully, you'll see that you've grown stronger and more centered, by giving others a chance to be who they are, giving both them and yourselves the space to live.

Accepting All Parts of Ourselves

It is not useful to label a part of ourselves good or bad. If we do, the "bad" part will start hiding, shame will appear and we'll withdraw from facing ourselves fully. All parts of ourselves, within and without, need to be met and known. Once we are acquainted with them, accept their presence, their power over us begins to fade away. Then we naturally let go of destructive aspects, integrate, and become whole. We become braver, freer, and more creative. Surprising solutions and insights appear. With a little persistence and patience it will only be a matter of a little while before your True Person starts emerging into the light.

This is the person who knows how to love, how to discover the "right relationship."

This is the person who makes friends easily. Isn't it time you let him/her free?

As you persist with these exercises you will notice many changes, day by day. People will seem less dangerous and distant. You will feel more loveable and awake. This is because your cardboard life is falling away, and it has been this false life that has separated you from love.

"Seaweed in the salad?
The cook must be in love!"

SECTION FOUR
A REAL CONVERSATION
(Encountering the Divine in One Another)

CHAPTER 14

Hearing the Call

Three Kinds of Conversations

There are three kinds of conversations we all have, with ourselves, with others, and with God (the Divine, Higher Self, or Ultimate Reality). These conversations often get mixed up. Rather than communicate with ourselves, we may only focus upon talking to others. Or, we may only turn to God, when our neighbor needs to hear what we have to say. Some forget about conversations with the Divine entirely, focusing only upon others or themselves. It is a great art to engage in all three kinds of conversations, to speak and to listen until all three voices become One.

Release from Loneliness

Often we do not communicate at all but are engaged in endless, repetitive conversations with ourselves. These are obsessions where the same thoughts go round and round, getting nowhere. Confusion, fixation and loneliness appear. So few know how to hear or speak their truths, let alone how to listen. And yet nothing less is needed for a release from the loneliness and the estrangement that grips us all. And nothing more is needed in order to be able to give and receive the love waiting for us.

We have a profound need to speak our truth and to be heard, and yet there are few who can really listen. And there are even fewer who know what it means to truly speak. Both of these activities seem dangerous.

Living as Strangers to Ourselves and Others

So we hide our true words, speak in riddles, give double messages, create innuendos and think we've had a conversation. We have not. As a result, most of us still live as strangers to others and to ourselves. And all the time we are longing to know and to be known.

If we do not speak, we cannot be answered.
We become strangers to others
And to ourselves.

Pillar of Love: To Be Truly Heard Is to Be Loved.

One of the greatest gifts we have been given is our ability to truly speak, reach out, and encounter one another. Yet after some conversations many feel more lonely, misunderstood, and shut down. Often the person we speak to is not able to hear what we're saying, or resonate with who we are. We blame ourselves then, but it is important to remember that true communication is rare.

"The World Addresses Us Daily."

Buber

A Conversation Between Us and The Divine

The universe speaks to us endlessly, but we do not hear what it is trying to say. We are not present, but caught in the grip of the repetitive stories we listen to and tell again and again.

These conversations are static and block out what is really being said and asked of us. The stories we endlessly repeat cause us to engage in conflict, create power struggles, defend ourselves vehemently. The noise of our lives can easily overpower the true communication that is flowing to us all the time.

But a true conversation brings the answer to everything. It is open and flowing, awake to all possibilities, holds back nothing back. A true conversation guides, informs, instructs and leaves all involved wiser and stronger.

The Universe Speaks to Us Endlessly

Martin Buber has said that the world is alive, it addresses us daily. Whatever happens to us is part of a conversation we are having with life, and awaits our response. It is amazing to realize that whatever happens is not a random conflagration of events. It is Life speaking to us, wanting something from us, stretching us, teaching us, hoping to engage us in a conversation from our depths. And waiting for us to make a reply!

Turning Point: Your Life Is Part of a Conversation Between You and The Divine

Can we begin to receive our lives as part of the conversation going on between us and the Divine? Let us start listening and looking at every moment as a conversation. It is thrilling to be addressed and to respond. But sadly, so often we are lost in dreams, sound asleep, not really able to listen, speak or hear.

But our gift of speech is precious and holy. It can help us uplift, inspire and truly draw close to others. We can use it to take down the veils that cover us from the experience of oneness and love.

Monologue and Dialogue

Martin Buber speaks of the difference between the world of monologue and dialogue. When we are engaged in monologue, although we seem to speaking to others, we are engaged only with ourselves. This is the world of I-It, where the other simply becomes an object for us. They are there to talk at, manipulate, or echo our beliefs.

As we speak we are paying attention to the voice within, and we do not hear what the other is saying or how we are affecting them. In this kind of conversation we are only concerned with our own opinions and making sure we are heard. Therefore, as we speak to others in this manner, and seemingly listen, we are only truly speaking to and listening to ourselves.

The World of I-Thou

In the world of I-Thou, the other becomes sacred to us. Who they are matters; we are fully here to listen and to hear. At that time we are engaging in dialogue, and when we do, the entire world opens up. We can make room to not only hear, but to respond to the other. We honor their experience, not add our own images and responses to what is being said. We also do not demand that the person fits into a preconceived category or speak in a certain kind of way.

In the world of I-Thou, the other becomes precious, real, close, hallowed. During dialogue the person is not a stranger, and we are not estranged from them or from ourselves.

Turning Point: Discover the World of Dialogue

"Words from the Heart
Go Into the Heart."

There is a wonderful way to learn how to speak and be heard completely, to open up to a true meeting with Life. Rebbe Nachman of Breslov, a great sage, recommends a simple but exceedingly powerful practice, to be done daily, called Hitbodedut.

Practice: Hitbodedut:

Speak to God Aloud as You Would to a Best Friend

In this beautiful, simple and powerful practice we seclude ourselves with God (Higher Self, Universe, Dharma, Ultimate Reality) and **Speak Out Loud** to Him/Her for as long as we can, each day.

Speak as if you were speaking to your **Best Friend**. If you can do it under a tree, or late at night, that is wonderful. If not, do it in your home, in the garden, in your bed, anywhere. It is important to seclude yourself, as if you were having an encounter with an intimate friend. It's just between the two of you.

Start talking for as long as you can each day and then build up. Eventually, some do it for hours at a time. Speak about whatever's on your mind truly, nothing fancy needed.

As the practice continues, you may see that all your words and actions are a form of an ongoing conversation with God.

Are We Talking to Ourselves?

On the surface, this can seem mad. What? Be alone, secluded, talk out loud, not only for a few minutes, but possibly hours? Isn't this the epitome of loneliness? Are we talking to ourselves? Not at all. In this incredibly simple practice, you will find the best listener you have ever met.

Discover the Best Listener

As the time rolls on and the conversation continues, a sense of being heard deepens and deepens. At a certain moment, you may not be able to utter another word. You are silenced. Suddenly you may feel how deeply you are being heard, known and received. Not only that, answers arise. Powerful, startling responses. Maybe not at that very moment, but sooner or later there are always answers and responses. How can that be? This is a wonderful koan.

Who Is the Speaker? Who Replies?

This practice brings everything into question. Who is the speaker? Who replies? When we realize that, taste it directly, our ability to know and speak to others, and to truly listen, opens up. The gates of our heart and life that have been locked swing wide open.

Turning Point: Do Not Be Deceived by Others

There is a wonderful Zen koan about speaking and answering, in which we find Master Zuigan calling out to himself each day.

"Master," he calls out.

"Yes," Zuigan answers.

"Are you there?"

"Yes, right here."

"Do not be deceived by others," Zuigan calls back.

"No, Master, I won't," he replies.

What an incredible dialogue. At first it may seem that Zuigan is a madman, calling to and answering himself. But he has gone way beyond this. Zuigan knows that we are all One, and the entire world hears and resonates to his call.

Zuigan addresses himself Master. Why? He is reminding himself that he can choose to wake up, be present and hear. He is making sure he remembers who he truly is. Zuigan is not a master who dominates others, but can have mastery over his ability to be present, to listen and respond.

Are You There?

Zuigan checks in and asks, are you there? This is an incredibly important question to ask ourselves all the time. Are we here? Are we available? Or are we simply lost in dreams? For a true conversation, we must be present, able to hear the call that is being made, and realize that we are being addressed. And we must respond.

"I'm here," Zuigan replies. This is similar to the Scriptures where man God asks Man, where are you? Or, where Man asks the same question of God.

"I am here," comes the answer. No one is alone."

Zuigan goes further in his precious encounter with himself, and with all of life. "Do not be deceived by others," he warns. This admonition is vital to allowing true conversations to take place. It's so easy to get deceived by the meaningless chatter of life and forget the power of a true word spoken directly, with full meaning, right from the heart.

"Forty-nine years
And not a word said."

Buddha

Pillar of Love: When We Are Truly Understood, We Feel Loved.

Turning Point: Become a True Listener

Some say true listening can cure a person. We usually listen only to part of ourselves and others. The rest is shut down. But no matter what we are denying, sooner or later it will be revealed. We need the ability to speak, to listen and to really hear what is being said. Actually, this is quite rare. Most of us live on the surface of our lives, caught up in automatic reactions which only make a situation or a problem more complicated and entrenched.

Pillar of Love: True Listening Is an Expression of Love.

Enter The World of the Speaker

To begin the process of true listening, simply become still, stop resisting and demanding anything and be fully present. You are listening for what the person is truly saying to you, what they need from you right now.

When we are in the process of deep listening, we open ourselves to the other, enter their world, and experience it along with them. We're beside them, walking along their way. The entire job of a listener is to learn how to become a wayfarer, to accompany whoever comes, wherever that person wants to go. We accompany them without judgments, directions, or reservation, in love, faith and trust.

The reward is to take many journeys with others, journeys you might never have embarked upon yourself. And to thank the person for having offered you that opportunity. It is a great gift you have been given. Handle it with care.

"Bring Your Words and Come to Me."

CHAPTER 15

Weeding the Garden
(Relationship Weeds and Tangles)

Relationship weeds and tangles inevitably arise in our relationships. They are created by lack of communication, misunderstandings and confusing messages of all kinds. What needs to be said often is not, or it is not comprehended. The misunderstanding grows and one partner finally declares the relationship over. They complain that the love has disappeared. The love hasn't disappeared. It was simply strangled by lack of true communication.

Weeding the Garden Day by Day
These tangles and weeds grow naturally in our relationships and need to be cleared day by day. The longer we let them stay, the sooner they fester and kill the love and trust that is trying to grow. There are many kinds of relationship weeds and tangles. Some are obvious, others are not.

We must learn to identify the weeds and tangles quickly. After that, it's a simple matter to pull them out. We'll go over different weeds and tangles in this chapter, so we can easily clear our relationship soil of resentment and make room for real communication to take place.

Naturally, real understanding and communication are needed to pull out the weeds and undo the tangles. Once that happens, love easily flowers. Let's explore the kinds of weeds and tangles that have grown in our relationships and see simple ways of pulling them out.

Exploring Relationship Weeds and Tangles

Confusing Conversations

We speak for many reasons, to give and receive information, to inquire, advise and learn. This is speaking for utilitarian purposes. Nothing wrong with that at all, it's natural and necessary.

But our conversations also take other turns. We can speak to dominate, cajole or control another. We can use words to intimidate, confuse or play with a person's heart. Sometimes we speak to gain recognition and approval. Other times we wish to win someone's love. We'll say anything we think they want to hear, if only they will think well of us.

Power trips can easily begin, with one person using another to aggrandize themselves. This is never part of a true conversation, but simply a case of manipulation, which always results in distress of some kind. Without real communication, hurt, disappointment and misunderstandings are bound to arise and develop.

Pillar of Love: Each Relationship Is a Profound Conversation.

Each relationship we have is a profound conversation, where we are called upon to be available, listen, and respond. Each person we meet is a new way to deepen the understanding and connection we can become capable of. As we do this we are building a bridge between us that we can walk across day by day.

As we build the bridge between us, all the conflicts we struggle with can be resolved.

All our doubts can be easily allayed. Solutions are found everywhere. There is one ingredient, however, that is crucial, the ability to *Truly Communicate Honestly.*

Turning Point: Celebrate Honesty

Call Me By My True Name

There's a beautiful poem by a great Vietnamese Zen master, Thich Nat Hanh, which says, "Call me by my true name." This means use language honestly. Call a thing what it is. Don't mix it up with something else. When we mix things up, we create mirages, get lost in delusions, confused and upset.

If you are in lust, don't call it love. If you have fantasies of being rescued and you meet a rescuer, call it rescue, not love. When you see that you want to be rescued, you'll soon understand that no person can truly do that forever. You won't blame the other for your pain, or be upset. It's inevitable that sooner or later a rescuer will tire of the role and you will have to face your fears. By calling this relationship by its true name, rescue, you become empowered to see what truly going on and deal with it wisely.

Practice: Clearing the Weeds

For a relationship not to be strangled by weeds, we must be able to speak, to listen and to hear what is being said. Naturally, there are various factors which get in our way. These factors become weeds, causing difficulties of all kinds.

In order to truly listen to another and really hear them, we must be still, stop judging what is being said, listen with an open mind. Our inner responses to what is being said often become static, making us unable to really hear the other. Let us explore some of the responses that could be blocking you in your relationship. Once you see what they are, it is a simple matter to pull out that weed.

Blocks to Truly Hearing

1) **Feelings about what is being said.** See if your feelings are getting in the way. If so, pay no attention to them while you are listening. Pay attention to the speaker instead.

2) **Judgments about the other person.** Notice what you think of the person or of what they are saying. Many of us do not listen to the other at all, just think of what we want to say in return. Say nothing in return. Just listen.

3) **A compulsion to express your opinions.** This isn't listening. It's bulldozing. Give them their time and chance to talk.

4) **Wanting to impress the other with how wise you are.** This isn't listening. It's making an impression. You don't have to impress them now. Let them take center stage. Make it all about them.

When we truly listen, we do not censor, criticize, correct, instruct, or insert our opinion. For now we put ourselves to the side. It is not what "we" think that is important, it's what we are finding out about them.

Blocks to Truly Speaking

It is not only listening that has its rough spots. Some of us aren't able to truly speak, either. Let us explore this now as well and see what gets in the way.

1) I Have No Idea What I Want to Say

A person who is communicating may have no idea what they really want to say.

They only vaguely know what they are feeling or wanting. They may experience all kinds of thoughts, fantasies and feelings, but seldom take the time to truly know what they truly think and want. What they think is communication then simply becomes an expression of their own confused, often conflicting thoughts.

2) Read My Mind

Some have no idea where they stand on an issue. They expect their partners to read their mind, naturally understand what they're wanting and give it to them, without their having to ask. When at times this magically happens, they think that this is love.

However, if their partner can't do this (as most cannot), the person starts to feel deprived and forlorn. They believe they are not understood and probably not loved.

3) Hiding the Truth: Mixed Messages

Another reason that communication is rare is that jumbled, mixed messages are very common. These messages often exist not to express what's going on, but to hide it. A grunt here, an action there, saying one thing and doing another all take the place of real communication.

But jumbled messages lead to jumbled responses. Mixed messages lead to confusion. A grunt here and there leads to nothing in your partner but confusion and a feeling of being alone.

Pillar of Love: When We Deceive Another We Are the One Who Gets Hurt.

4) Not Telling the Whole Story

Sometimes, unwittingly, we tell part of a story or just imply what's really going on.

The rest is left to be imagined. We may assume our partner knows what we're thinking. Wrong. This frequently leads to misunderstandings and all kinds of fantasies and fears on the partner's part.

Turning Point: Give Up Deception, Lies and Hidden Agendas

Deception, lies and hidden agendas are the most poisonous weeds because they pull the trust right out of a relationship. We may think we're lying to someone else, but lies and deceptions cause the greatest damage to ourselves. The more we indulge in it, the less we are able to even trust ourselves.

Practice: Say Exactly What Needs to Be Said.

Tell the whole story. Make sure your partner hears you. Otherwise, it is very likely they will come to a set of conclusions that are different from yours.

5) The Disappearance of Trust

When trust disappears in a relationship, the entire fabric of the relationship crumbles. Suspiciousness, possessiveness and jealousy develop. A person's sense of self-worth disappears. No one can feel loved or loving in a relationship where lies, deception and hidden agendas have not been brought to the light and cleared up.

6) Refusing to Communicate

Refusing to communicate is itself a form of communication. It says you're not interested, available or willing to be there and share what is happening. This can be a form of withholding from the partner or punishing them. We have endless ways of hiding from and sabotaging love, putting barriers in the way. By withdrawing in a relationship, or refusing to say what's on your mind, you are shutting doors to your own happiness and well-being.

Refusing to Communicate Is a Communication

Being with a partner who refuses to communicate can become very exhausting and draining. It can also be a form of passive-aggression. The person who refuses to communicate is angry, but unwilling to talk about what's going on. Instead they express their anger through silence and making promises that they do not keep. This can drive their partner crazy, always trying to get the person to talk. The person acts as though they haven't done anything, that all the difficulties are happening because their partner wants too much.

7) Not Asking For What Is Wanted

Some feel ashamed to ask for what they want. Some believe what they want should come automatically. Others may think they don't deserve to get what they desire. Others are afraid to ask, in case the partner says no. These people cannot accept refusal and see it as personal rejection (which it is not).

Practice: Ask For What You Want

Ask for what you want and need and be willing to accept an honest answer. Your partner may or may not be able to give it to you. Because they can't does not mean they do not love you. It simply means they cannot say yes to that particular request.

It is unreasonable to expect that our partners must fulfill all our requests.

Turning Point: You Can't Say Yes if You Can't Say No

If a person cannot say no, they cannot say yes. Their yes is not a truly yes from the bottom of their heart, but acquiescence and compulsion. Usually they are just doing what they feel you want.

No Is Not a Rejection of You, It Is an Expression of What They Are Capable Of. By accepting another person's limits and boundaries and not rejecting them, you are on the road to a true relationship, based upon the deepest respect.

Responsible Communication

We cannot truly communicate unless we respect both ourselves and the other. Responsible communication is not about blaming another or projecting our judgments onto them. If we are angry, it is not about saying how awful they are, or what they did to us.

Responsible communication is simply and honestly taking responsibility for how we feel and communicating it that way. Instead of saying, "You are horrible," we say, "Right now I'm feeling disappointed."

We take responsibility for our needs, thoughts and feelings, and communicate them simply and directly. When we speak and express what we are feeling we are careful to speak in way so that the other does not get hurt. That way the person you are talking to is more able to hear you as well.

Turning Point: Hurting Another Is Not Communication, It Is Attack

True communication is realizing that we all have different needs, wants, abilities and rhythms. We create a space for each person to be who they are and to share it with us willingly.

Receiving Feedback

It is very important to let your partner know that you have truly heard them. Feedback is essential. At some point, let the other know what you've heard them say. This will have amazing effects. First of all, they'll know you've been listening. Very often they'll make some important correction in what you say, preventing misunderstanding from growing.

You may have heard one thing while they meant another. It will be very illuminating and sometimes surprising as well. Other times, when you truly have "gotten" what was intended, there will be a wonderful feeling on the part of your partner of having been really heard. Your partner will feel as though they are not alone, that you are truly with them. This itself is experienced as love.

Practice: Identifying Your Relationship Weeds and Tangles

1) **Write down weeds you've allowed to grow** in your relationship. Decide to clear them today. You can start with something small, perhaps some-

thing you've been disappointed about, or something you've forgotten to say thank you for.

2) **Sit down with your partner and take the smallest weed out first.** You will be amazed how refreshing it will be to sit down with your partner and clear the deck. Once this misunderstanding or secret has been brought to light, calmly, with kindness, you'll become closer and easily see what is needed next.

3) **Let Go of Past Grievances.** Some people hold onto what has been said at one point in time and never let it go. The ability to forgive may be just as simple as realizing that what was true a year ago may not be true now. True communication requires the ability to remain in the present moment and to let the past be over when it's done.

4) **Listen to Everything They Want to Say.** Most people only listen to part of what the other is saying. They automatically censor what they do not want to hear. They have an idea of who they want the person to be and how he is supposed to behave. If they hear something they don't like, immediately they think of ways to change it.

Just listen. Listen to all of it. Believe what you hear. The person is revealing themselves to you. Don't figure ways of fixing him up. Just honor his truth. Listen with both ears.

Pillar of Love: Our True Happiness Comes from Being True to Ourselves.

Honesty is the Healer

"Humankind cannot bear
Very much reality."

T. S. Eliot

Turning Point: Celebrate Honesty

In order to communicate honestly, you have to accept honesty from others and also from yourself. The assumption is everybody's going to be honest. The truth is, few people are. Many can't, or won't.

The ability to accept honesty from others grows as we are able and willing to be honest with ourselves and as we realize that our true security does not come from the approval of others, but from being true to ourselves.

A Day of Reality Is a Day of Healing

"Truth heals. Honesty is the healer."

CHAPTER 16

A Real Meeting

"There is nothing in life
More important
Than a meeting with
The Friend."

Rumi

Real Meetings

What is a real meeting? How do we know when it is happening? A real meeting is different from a usual encounter. It stops us on the spot and takes us home to our center. There is no more wandering in confusion; we no longer feel lost and alone. A deep connection happens, as we feel directly that the two of us are one. When this takes place our sense of disconnection vanishes and our sense of belonging grows deep roots.

Some say it is necessary to prepare an entire life in order to be ready for a real meeting. It's good to prepare, but when the time comes, real meetings happen spontaneously. They can happen for a moment, or can last awhile. They can happen between two people, or between a person and a child, an animal, plant or bird flying by. We cannot demand that a real meeting happens. But we can learn how to invite it in.

Inviting a Real Meeting

Our hearts have a language of their own. The voice of the heart is always eager to be heard, though we usually try to keep it down. Sometimes it simply bursts forth. When it does a real meeting can take place.

Let us see what is required for a real meeting to take place. The most important ingredients are two people who are real and who are willing to be here in the present moment. This means that each person is willing, for the moment, to let go of their need to control the interaction. They even forget about themselves, about being right, wonderful, or special in any way.

They are not using the relationship to develop their fantasy. They are simply willing to be present each moment and to allow anything to happen, exactly as it wants to. One simply has to accept all as it comes and as it is. Nothing extra has to be said or done. Instead, simply be there, open and fully available to whatever is going on. This will bring deep comfort and presence, allowing the meeting to unfold.

Turning Point: Let Full Communication Stream Forth

This kind of meeting is tremendously liberating. When it happens, some begin to laugh out loud or even cry. Most of us have experienced a taste of this kind of meeting at one time or another. It is everyone's natural birthright.

Martin Buber describes this kind of meeting beautifully in his essay "Between Man and Man." It involves two strangers who meet in the early evening on a deserted platform, waiting for a train. They know nothing of one another. The train arrives and the two enter the train, sit down next to one another, open their newspapers, read them, and do not speak.

Suddenly and unexpectedly, full communication streams from one person to the next. During this time each knows everything about the other. They feel as close to one another as to their very selves. Both hearts have opened and spoken, although not a word has been said.

Lifting a Spell

Buber says it is as though a spell is lifted and the reserve which we usually hold over ourselves is released. As we enter into a real meeting, we move into another level of communication; some call it communion. It is encountering the divine within one another, being in touch with that which is greater than us and yet speaks and lives through us.

> *"When you really look for me, you*
> *Will see me instantly,*
> *You will find me in the tiniest*
> *House of time.*
> *Kabir says – student, tell me,*
> *Where is God?*
> *He is the breath inside the breath."*

> *Kabir*

The Sound of Silence

Sitting at the Zendo

One night a student went to the zendo and sat down on the cushion next to a dear dharma friend whom she particularly cared for. What does it mean to sit with a friend? It doesn't mean to sit down to chat, but to just sit still in the silence beside one another, breathing together.

Sitting in this manner, we are not seeking anything from the other, just sharing the moment, and our precious breath. As we do so, division ends.

"Deep calls unto deep."

The zendo is a place where silence is treasured, where we listen to silence speak. Of course the chatter of our minds does not stop instantly, or perhaps ever at all. It is just that we do not pay attention to it, or believe what it says. Sooner or later, the chatter dims in the background, and the silence becomes the forefront of our lives.

This silence is not the refusal of communication—just the opposite. It is the willingness to become truly still so we can hear the deeper call. Deep within each of us our heart is speaking, calling out, though usually it cannot be heard. As we stop moving, grabbing, running and scheming, the silence takes over and we become able to hear the Silent Sound.

Practice: Make Friends with the Silence

It is impossible to hear what is being said when you are filled with static and noise. It is important to be able to enter the silence, be at home in it, in order to allow yourself to be available to what is being said. In true silence we can hear everything.

Turning Point: Communication Streams Forth in the Silence

Practice: Being at Home in the Silence

Zazen is the practice of entering the silence, feeling safe and at home there, and deeply listening to what it has to say. As we sit still without moving, face the wall, we allow the breath to breathe us. Distractions are eliminated, and as we sit we inevitably become aware of all that is going on within. We see that our thoughts, images, memories and hopes come and go, and learn not to cling to them or depend upon them. Instead we just remain present for the endless array of life. What wonderful training for listening, and being there for all who come our way.

Zazen retreats are scheduled where we have the opportunity to listen more deeply. During a retreat the seating is arranged and we sit next to the same person for the entire time. We do not speak to one another or look at each other the entire time. We simply pay attention to our own practice.

And yet, after the retreat is over, a profound bond grows between those who have shared the silence this way. And even though not a word has been said, many feel as if they know all about their partners, are profoundly connected, way beyond words.

How has this happened? Communications streams forth in the silence. Words are often simply a cover-up for what really needs to be heard and said. As we learn to listen to, live in and hear the silence, our world totally turns around.

Practice: Inviting a Real Meeting

In a real meeting the other reveals themselves to you in a completely different way. Of course, as this takes place, you simultaneously and unconsciously reveal yourself to them as well. And to yourself. A real meeting shows us who we are and how deeply fulfilling life is.

Become Accustomed to the Silence and What It Has to Say to You

Become at home in the silence, listen to it deeply, rather than to all the voices that scream out loud and constantly demand our attention. Don't let yourself become distracted by the fireworks and clamor of daily life. Don't become intoxicated by the glitter of a person, but listen deeply to who they truly are, and what their heart wants to say.

This is simply a matter of redirecting your attention, guarding it, not getting caught. Spending some time being in the silence each day helps grow the ability to do this. It is time well spent beyond what anyone can imagine.

Allowing True Communication to Stream Forth

Most important is a receptive heart, a desire to go deeper into the ocean of life and taste the gifts waiting for you there. When your heart opens, it releases not only its treasures, love and wisdom, but makes a place for others to join you there. Although we feel the opposite is true, when we open our hearts we are safest, filled with appreciation, beauty and a safe home for all to come to.

Practice: Opening Your Heart

Practice opening your hearts. Do this by noticing when you are closed up, suspicious, doubtful, defensive. Just notice it and how that makes you feel. The awareness starts the process of softening. Then, breathe deeply into your heart and tell it it's safe to open up. See for yourself that it is.

What streams forth from your heart will happen in the silence, and yet those who have ears to hear, will hear. And you will feel the expansion of your life in so many ways.

Turning Point: Encountering the Divine in One Another

As life goes on, many long for a real meeting, to feel the Divine presence in their lives. They begin to realize that the emptiness within them can only be filled by contact with the Timeless. There are many forms of welcoming this encounter, which could also be thought of as forms of prayer. Some say prayer or encountering is its own answer. The joy and fullness we receive as we pray is the deepest fulfillment.

The Many Faces of Prayer

Just as it is natural for the human being to seek friendship, it is natural to connect with the Divine. In the state of prayer we are relating ourselves to something larger than our own personal selves. We are also inviting this larger sense of life to permeate our entire being and life. Offering real meetings all through the day.

Prayer connects one with the Divine. It can take endless forms. For many, prayer is a repetition of phrases; others feel their prayers are only successful if they receive their desired outcomes. This kind of prayer is not necessarily an overflowing, which comes from feeling full.

Other ways of praying include giving gifts, chanting, dancing, meditating or working in the garden. For some the way they behave in relationships itself is the prayer. And their relationship is their temple.

Others would suggest that prayer itself allows us to become all we were meant to be. They would say that true prayer is an activity through which man reaches for the highest in himself and allows his/her separateness to fall away. This kind of prayer unlocks our heart. We see that prayer is the very process of becoming one with all beings, and of regarding our lives with reverence and awe. In this case, prayer becomes our very way of being in the world.

Whatever the source and form of your prayer, it is necessary to take the divine with you into everyday life, for it to become manifested in all action and words, become concrete, vivid and thoroughly real.

This is a state of mind that beautifies its surroundings wherever it goes, and which makes the person and all they meet trustworthy, enlivened and blessed.

Turning Point: Become Trustworthy Wherever You May Be

Being Trustworthy

The world has never been in such a great need of a truly trustworthy people. Trustworthy people uphold the world by restoring faith in others, themselves and the divine. This is a form of the "living God," which is always alive, changing, loving. This attitude brings a person to their true spiritual connection and allows them to grow from there.

To live fully requires courage and faith. As we become authentic and available, trust and faith naturally grow. It cannot be otherwise.

"We live under a power which negates and destroys us, which seeks to oppress and crush us."

Paul Tillich

This power arises from the conditioning and fear that have been generated over centuries. But even a little bit of truth dispels a lot of darkness; even a little bit of trustworthiness and real caring go a very long way.

Turning Point: Invite the Larger Sense of Life into Your Day

Practice: Turn Your Daily Activities into Prayer

*"The Most Important Thing
Is What You Are Doing Right Now."*

1) View whatever you are doing as an offering to the Divine.

Take your time with whatever you are doing. Offer it as a prayer, a gift. Don't be concerned with the outcome, or who will or will not appreciate it, just do it with your full heart.

2) Don't cut corners.

"Leave No Traces."

Do everything through and through, leave nothing out. Give your whole self to it, and it will give its whole self to you. In Zen we say, "Leave no Traces." Nothing undone, no straggly ends behind.

3) Say yes to what is needed of you.

Give up the withholding, judging mind. When we learn to say yes unrestrainedly, that itself is a beautiful prayer.

4) Give thanks for the opportunity to share what you have.

We think it's a great thing to receive, and it is, but it's even more wonderful to be able to share who we are and what we have. Don't wait for another time to give it. Give it all now.

Practice: Opening the Gates of the Divine

The gates of the divine are right within our heart, and as we practice the ways of love, they strengthen and open naturally.

Turning Point: Offer All an Invitation to Live

Some people are inspiring and life giving; others create a sense of defeat and doom. When events do not go as planned they become fearful and sad. Some then say life has lost its purpose and they are lost. But why do we think we know what is best or what the ultimate outcome of the events will be? We cannot depend upon circumstances to be well and happy, but upon the strength and wisdom within.

Never Give Up on a Person – Never Give Up on Yourself

Here is an instruction to use in everyday life which comes from *Lojong*. (*Lojong* is part of Tibetan Buddhist teaching. This practice is beautifully described by Pema Chodron.)

How easy it is to give up on others, on the Divine and on ourselves, when our expectations aren't met. The minute this happens remind yourself of this instruction and take a deep breath. Return to the situation with patience, compassion and watchfulness.

We are helped in this practice by staying still through all kinds of conditions, remaining steadfast in the face of everything. We do not give up on anything, but are able to learn from what is happening, and be guided to make a beneficial response.

Practice: Fall Down and Get Up Again

In Zen we say fall down seven times, get up eight times. It's natural and inevitable to fall down; this is how we grow strong. A child would never learn to walk if they didn't fall and get up many times. Each time we get up, we are responding to An Invitation To Live, to try again. We are demonstrating deep faith in the process that runs the Universe, knowing that we are part of it, and can only flourish in the long run.

Courage is necessary, and so is resilience. There is a deep law of life which will guide us infallibly, when we allow it. And when we choose to be loving and just.

"Are you looking for me? I am in the next seat. My shoulder is against yours. You will not find me in stupas, Churches, shrines, zendos, not in Legs winding around your neck, nor In eating nothing but vegetables."

Kabir

Brenda Shoshanna, Ph.D., is a psychologist, author, playwright, speaker and long-term practitioner of Zen and Judaism. Her work is dedicated to integrating the teachings of East and West and making them real in our everyday lives. She has offered many talks and workshops on all aspects of psychological and spiritual development, relationships, spiritual counseling, and living an authentic life.

**The website for the book is
www.totalrelationships.com.**

Some of Brenda's talks and workshops include:
The Unshakable Road to Love (Value-Centered
Relationships)
Making Your Life into a Zen Koan (Acting Zen)
Real Spiritual Counseling

www.brendashoshanna.com
www.totalrelationships.com
zenplaynow.com
realspiritualcounseling.com

Made in the USA
Las Vegas, NV
27 June 2023

73962763R00115